THE NASCAR ART OF SAM BASS

THE  NASCAR® ART OF

Sam Bass

BY SAM BASS

WITH BRAD BOWLING

 **DAVID BULL** PUBLISHING

Library of Congress Control Number: 2004110214
ISBN: 1 893618 32 3

David Bull Publishing, logo, and colophon are trademarks of David Bull Publishing, Inc.

Book and cover design:
Tom Morgan, Blue Design, Portland, Maine

Printed in Hong Kong

10 9 8 7 6 5 4 3 2 1

David Bull Publishing
4250 East Camelback Road
Suite K150
Phoenix, AZ 85018

602-852-9500
602-852-9503 (fax)

www.bullpublishing.com

Previous page: "True Success," 1998, 25" x 31"
True Value commissioned this painting as part of its national promotion to honor NASCAR's 50th anniversary.

This page: "Won & Done," 2004, 35" x 27"
This painting commemorates Dale Earnhardt Jr.'s 2004 Daytona 500 victory and was released just as this book went to press.

Next page: "7 & 7," 1995, 22" x 30"
The only two drivers in NASCAR's history to claim seven Winston Cup championships, Richard Petty and Dale Earnhardt, are celebrated in this watercolor illustration.

Contents

ACKNOWLEDGMENTS

Thanks to everyone who has ever encouraged me or supported my artwork over the years…I love what I do.

To drivers and team owners
Davey Allison, Neil Bonnett, Richard Childress, Dale Earnhardt, Jr., Ray Evernham, Bill Elliott, Armando Fitz, Harry Gant, Jeff Gordon, Rick Hendrick, Jimmie Johnson, Matt Kenseth, Bobby Labonte, Terry Labonte, Mark Martin, Kyle Petty, Richard Petty, Felix Sabates, Tony Stewart, and Darrell Waltrip.

To my friends at NASCAR
Paul Brooks, Mark Dyer, Brian France and the NASCAR family, Amber O'Neil, George Pyne, and Liz Schlosser.

To track owners and managers
Jerry Gappens, Eddie Gossage, Paul Sawyer, Bruton Smith, and H.A. "Humpy" Wheeler.

To my clients
David Allen, Don Hawk, Johnny Hayes, Scott Hayes, Joe Hedrick, John Isley and Billy James ("John Boy & Billy"), Hank Jones, John Kenny, Cindy Lynskey, John McKenzie, Don Miller, Bill Nystrom, Sue Seaglund, Edd Stonich, and Fred Wagenhals.

Additional personal thanks
Tom Cotter, René Cobb Damewood, Johnny and Barbara Dean, Kelley Earnhardt, Martha Earnhardt, Bruce Ellis, George Fetrow, Betty Griggs, Russ and Joanne Hamilton, Sandra Ketchie, Nigel Kinrade, Mark Kowalski, Bruce Mueller, Tom Mueller, Chris Politis, Robbie Robertson, Matt Smart, Jeff Scanlan, Ralph Sheheen, Barbara Tisseratt, Mike Turek, Cathy Watkins, Carolyn Whitlock, Lori Worley, my wife's parents Jim and Norma Will, my uncles Doug, Bill, Roy, and Jim, my staff Patti, Heather, Scott, Michael, Phillip, Missy and Stephanie, and all of my friends at Gibson.

Special thanks to those who shaped the very foundation of the career I enjoy today, and hope to have for as long as God lets me: Bobby Allison, Dale and Teresa Earnhardt, Robb Griggs, Clarence Joyner, and Rusty Wallace.

And to Susan Russo for her belief that I could make this whole thing happen, her tireless efforts to keep it going, and for her unconditional friendship through it all. Here is the book you've always wanted to see me do!

Sam Bass
Charlotte, June 2004

DEDICATION

To Denise, Kendyl, Mark, Mom, and Rick,

Thanks for all of your love and support while I've chased my dream,
especially for our time together that you've willingly sacrificed
along the way as I worked on projects. I promise to make it up to you.
I love you all, and could never thank you enough.

Celebrating 20 Great Years of the *Coca-Cola* 600

2002 • **1996** • **1985** • **1987** • **1989** • **1991**
1994 • **1993** • **2001** • **1990** • **1995**
1986 • **2004** Coca-Cola 600 20 YEARS OF RACING • **1992** • **1998**
1988 • **2003** • **2004** • **1997** • **1999** • **2000**

Program Cover Art by Sam Bass Illustration & Design, Inc. ©2004

NASCAR   www.sambass.com

FOREWORD

by H. A. "Humpy" Wheeler, President and General Manager, Lowe's Motor Speedway

Can the work of one man really affect the image of an entire industry? If he has the talent and drive of Sam Bass, the answer is yes.

Back in the early eighties I visited a motorsports art gallery in midtown Manhattan, where I was astonished to find not a single piece of stock car art. Formula 1 and European sports-car racing with a smattering of Indy cars made up the subjects in the gallery. This disturbed me immensely. How could the fastest growing sport in America not be represented in this swank gallery?

The answer was quite simple. There was only a smattering of artists around NASCAR and most of them were commercial in nature (they had to make a living!).

I began to encourage NASCAR art by buying and exhibiting pieces, and along came an aspiring artist from Virginia named Sam Bass. I looked at his portfolio and saw something special in his touch. I asked him to create a painting for the cover of the Coca Cola 600 race program and—35 or so covers later—the rest is history.

Not only is Sam's talent magnificent, he is a true Virginia gentleman who always has time for everybody, whether his admirers are in grandstands, galleries, wheelchairs, or hospital beds. When my grandchildren grow up I want them to be just like Sam.

Sam is one of the most prolific artists in America. His work spans everything from graphic paint schemes for our sport's best race cars to portraits of our most famous drivers. Most race fans probably don't realize it, but much of the color and presentation they see at the track and on television was either created or influenced by Sam, which is illustrated in this great book.

Because his work has given today's NASCAR its look and texture to a degree no one else has managed, I can sum up his importance to the sport by saying, the pope needed Michelangelo and we needed Sam.

"Coca-Cola 20th Anniversary," 2004, 30"x 24"
Coca-Cola commissioned this painting to celebrate its sponsorship of the classic 600-mile Memorial Day weekend race held at Lowe's Motor Speedway.

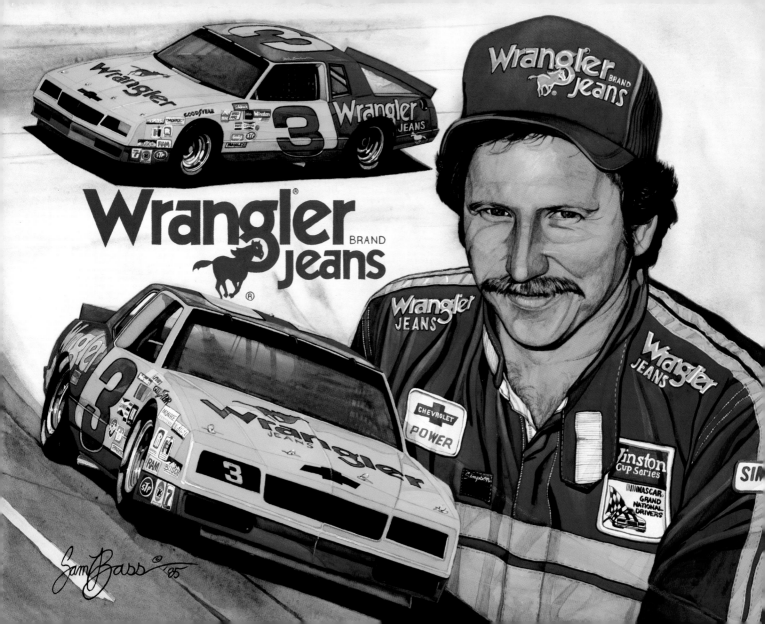

INTRODUCTION

On a chilly day in February 1985, I found myself walking through the hardscrabble infield at Richmond before final practice, looking for Dale Earnhardt. I had produced a painting that featured Dale and his Wrangler-sponsored car, and the people at Wrangler were interested in buying it for what seemed like a huge sum of money to me back then—$300. But before I sold the painting, it was important to me to first get Dale's approval. I was 24, just out of college, and though I didn't know it at the time, I was on the threshold of beginning my career as a NASCAR artist, which I had wanted so badly.

I found Dale sitting in his Blazer with his wife, Teresa, in the area where the teams and drivers parked their cars. I mustered up my courage, walked over, and tapped on the window. Dale looked at me with an expression that seemed to ask, "Whatcha got?" I said, "Dale, I have something that your sponsor is very interested in purchasing from me," and I held up the painting. I told him how much Wrangler wanted to pay me for it. Then I said, "I didn't want to sell it to them without your blessing on the painting and without knowing how much of the money I would need to give to you." Although back then there wasn't the formal licensing process that is common today, I knew that if I was going to sell something with his image on it, I pretty much needed to make sure he liked it and to work out a business arrangement with him.

By the way that Dale looked at the painting and smiled, I could tell that he was pleased by my efforts. He was always the type of person who would ask the people he was with for their comments, and I experienced this for the first time when he looked over to Teresa and asked her what she thought. She agreed that it looked good. Dale said, "Fine, go ahead and sell it." And that was it. Dale didn't want any money from the sale, but I was glad I had offered; it demonstrated that I had a professional approach.

Dale Earnhardt had approved my painting! I was ecstatic. Presenting the painting to him and getting his impressions was something I needed to do to establish myself. But what was even more important to me was that Dale knew I was committed to doing my best possible work and that the money was almost irrelevant to me. I was planning to be around the sport for a long time—being a NASCAR artist was all I dreamed about—so I wanted Dale and other drivers to know that this was my career and that they were very important to me.

I think that from that moment forward, both Dale and Teresa sensed the sincerity in what I was trying to do with my work. Amazingly, in the almost 20 years that I worked with Dale, we never had a contract or legal document. Our relationship was based on trust and the knowledge that I was trying to do my best and to please him with whatever the project was that I was doing. And he was a tough man to please—he and Teresa both knew what they wanted, and they would challenge me to give it to them. But there was no greater sense of accomplishment than in achieving that.

As I was starting out, it was thanks to Dale and to other drivers such as Bobby Allison and Rusty Wallace, and their sponsors, that I was able to become a full-time artist. From childhood, I've always enjoyed drawing and designing. Now I'm fortunate to do what I love professionally, and to be involved in all aspects of artwork—from the fine art approach to the graphic design of cars and uniforms, to logos and track mascots. To me all of it is appealing, and it's been my joy to experience so much of it firsthand.

A lot of people ask me about the technical parts of my work. They want to know just how it all happens and what kind of materials I use. Answering those questions seems like a good place to start to talk about the technical aspects of my work. When I graduated from using crayons as a child, I began working in watercolors, mostly cheap kids' stuff at the time. Today I work in a lot of different media, but primarily still watercolor, both opaque (which is called gouache) and transparent, even though they can be very unforgiving if you make mistakes. With oils and acrylics, you can cover up mistakes by simply painting right over them.

Watercolor paint won't cover in the same way, but it works better for my purposes. I like it because it dries quickly and saves me time. Oil paintings take too long to dry, although I've done a few in my career. Given the nature of this business, where everything has to be done in a hurry, oil painting is just not conducive to staying on schedule. Matching the intensity of race car paint schemes can be difficult with watercolor, but I've developed my own technique in which I use very little water and paint with almost pure color.

Generally I start a painting by creating a very loose pencil sketch of an original idea, which I then develop until it's as tight and detailed as I need it to be. Sometimes I'll trace the finished pencil sketch and do all the final tweaking on transfer paper, then place that over my sheet of illustration board and/or watercolor paper that will receive the actual illustration. That way, all the mistakes that occur normally in a drawing as I'm working on it have been eliminated by the time I put it on the fresh white piece of paper that's going to receive the inking and watercolor. This keeps the sheet of paper much cleaner and nicer by eliminating a lot of the working and reworking areas. If I'm in a hurry, I might go straight from the original drawing to the finished painting on the same sheet of paper.

I also experiment with other media. I have done a number of pen and ink drawings, which I enjoy quite a bit, as the black and white aspect gives a contrast that really brings the subject to life. Graphite pencil drawings have a lot of appeal for me, too, especially after I've done several watercolors in a row. Sometimes it's just fun to change media to break things up. I also like using colored pencils, which I occasionally combine with Magic Marker and opaque watercolors. Sometimes I'll even use acrylics on top of watercolor to create super-bright highlights.

LICENSE TO PAINT

From the very first painting I offered for sale, I have worked with my subjects to secure their permission and licensing arrangements. When I was starting my career, most drivers made their money from sponsors and from competition; only a handful had any income from licensed souvenirs. Today the opposite it true. It would be hard to find anyone on the Nextel circuit without some licensing agreements. The licensing of a driver's name or image is big business in NASCAR.

The law is very clear about reproducing a sports star's image or name on a hat or T-shirt without permission; however, traditionally statutes have been vague concerning the painting or photographing of a celebrity—even if there is financial gain on the part of the artist or photographer. Just recently a federal appellate court in Ohio ruled in favor of Tuscaloosa, Ala., sports artist Rick Rush and his limited edition prints of golfer Tiger Woods. The court views the offering of the prints as "an artist's creation seeking to express a message" with First Amendment protection.

Be that as it may, I've never wanted to paint someone so badly that I would do it against his wishes.

Because of my background in commercial artwork, licensing came naturally to me. I also knew that cooperating with a team, sponsor, or driver would bring me 100 times more business than doing things without their permission. How many limited-edition prints do you think drivers would have autographed for me if I had taken that approach? I have more respect for them than that.

Initially arrangements amounted to a quick meeting and a handshake, but today's legal climate requires contracts of 30 pages or more. I've been careful that the folks at NASCAR understood my level of commitment to the sport and to its history. It was important to me that they knew I was in this business as a fan and for the long run. In the mid '90s I met with George Pyne and Liz Schlosser from NASCAR and spoke to them at length about my plans for the business and for a licensing program with the sanctioning body itself. My request was that I become the first officially licensed artist of NASCAR, because I had tremendous faith in stock car racing's future. They graciously accepted my offer, and have been incredibly supportive over the years.

Above: "Proven Winners," 1990. This is one of a series of paintings commissioned by AC Spark Plugs between 1989 and 1994 to promote its team of drivers.

CHAPTER 1:
BOBBY ALLISON

Bobby Allison has been so instrumental in my career—such a motivating force—that I sometimes wonder how differently my life would have turned out had he not been so supportive of my early work. It was his perseverance and ability to overcome adversity that made Bobby such a natural role model for me at a young age. The fact that he was an amazing driver was an added bonus.

In February 1981 my wife, Denise, who was my fiancée then, and I attended a Bobby Allison fan club banquet. With me was a painting I had created for Bobby of his Tuf-Lon Pontiac Winston Cup car, and I was ecstatic about the fact that I would be presenting it to him during the dinner. Bobby seemed genuinely pleased that I had gone to the trouble of painting something for him, and I was overjoyed to get such a positive reaction from him. It was my first full-blown watercolor painting, and I considered it to be fine art at the time.

I discovered that night how much I enjoyed being in front of the public and having people talk to me about my artwork. Up to that time, my paintings had mostly been enjoyed only by me, my family, and my friends, but my admiration for Bobby made it possible to display an image I had created to people I had never met. Painting is a very lonely pursuit, but when those other race fans started telling me how much they liked my work, I realized it could have unexpected benefits.

Performing in a band on a stage gives you an immediate response from the crowd that lets you know if they like what they are hearing. I know this because my love of music and the guitar has put me in that scenario many times. Being an artist, on the other hand, is like being a marathon runner who has no idea how well he's doing until the race is over. The difference between the two was never so clear to me until that night at the banquet.

And the whereabouts of the painting that caused such an epiphany in the mind of a fresh high school graduate? I hope it is still in Bobby's collection. All I have to document the moment is a really poor Polaroid snapshot that, to me, is priceless.

"The Best Comes Shining Through"

17" x 22", 1988

enjoyed doing paintings for the souvenir programs at the Richmond International Raceway because it's my home track (only about 20 minutes from Hopewell, where I grew up) and because owner Paul Sawyer was such a generous and enthusiastic supporter of my early career.

"The Best Comes Shining Through" was the program cover for Richmond's Miller 400 in 1989. Considering the race's sponsor, it was not surprising that I was asked to feature Bobby Allison and the No. 12 Miller High Life Buick. Abusing my artistic license a little, I chose to show Bobby celebrating his Daytona victory from 1988 hoisting a Miller beer can in triumph. I thought it would be cool to also show his car crossing the Richmond start/finish line.

This painting was an early visual résumé of my graphic services: I designed both the RIR logo and the Miller car paint scheme, so the painting was a good example of my design and illustration abilities.

"The Real Thing!"

19" x 25", 1991

The early '70s was when the world of NASCAR really opened up to me as a fan, especially when it came to the Coca-Cola Chevrolet Monte Carlo that Bobby drove to 10 wins in 1972 racing for Junior Johnson.

The sight of that Coca-Cola car flying around Richmond's Fairground Raceway in 1972—the first Winston Cup race I attended in person—was a thrill that had an effect on the rest of my life. Bobby and Richard Petty were waging war on the track as each drove the wheels off of his car, battling for the championship.

To this day I believe that that Coca-Cola Monte Carlo of his was one of the most beautiful race cars in NASCAR history.

Sometime in the early 1990s, Robb Griggs, who was the owner of *NASCAR Scene* and *NASCAR Illustrated* at the time, asked me to paint the '72 race car for a special installment of his company's *American Classics* book series.

This painting took quite a bit of time because I wanted to get every detail perfect.

Unfortunately, after I worked more than 75 hours on the illustration, it somehow got left out of the book. A few years later I licensed "The Real Thing!" through Coca-Cola—my first time gaining licensee status with them—for a limited print run of 250, and I invited Bobby to be a guest at our gallery's open house. That day is one of the highlights of my life, having Bobby spend a couple of hours with my friends and customers, graciously autographing prints for fans.

"Winning Tradition!"

22" x 28", 1992

For the 1992 Unocal dinner at Charlotte Motor Speedway, Humpy Wheeler challenged me to create an image that would really get an emotionally charged response from its recipient, 1991 Coca-Cola 600 winner Davey Allison.

My first thought was that I needed to incorporate Darvey's father, Bobby, into the painting in a subtle way that still managed to make clear that the racing legacy was being passed from father to son. I portrayed Davey driving in the tracks of his father by having the No. 28 Havoline car reflect the No. 12 Miller High Life car. Bobby, who had won the same event in 1984, holds his trophy and watches over Davey's victory circle celebration.

My wife, Denise, and I were sitting in the audience in the front row at The Speedway Club when Davey was presented with the painting. He looked at it, then at me, and said, "Sam, this is awesome!" It was an amazing feeling to hear such praise from the painting's subject. I knew I had done exactly what Humpy had asked me to do.

Later I learned that when Davey and his wife, Liz, were building their new home in Alabama, Davey made sure that the painting was placed directly in front of his favorite chair so that whenever he was relaxing or watching TV, he was virtually staring at the painting I did for him.

It was a very special evening for me as a Bobby Allison fan, having watched Davey grow up, to know that he treasured that painting. That means the world to me now.

Over the years I've had a lot of really great opportunities to work with drivers who are just entering the Busch and Nextel series.

Once Davey was on his feet in the sport, he asked me to design his business card, which I thought was a really unique request. It was, at the time, one of the few things I had not been asked to design for a driver.

I wish there were a lot more stories to tell about Davey; unfortunately, about a year after I presented him with "Winning Tradition!" we lost him in a tragic helicopter accident.

The MAXX card set incorporates innovative design that works whether the card is viewed straight up or on its side. The driver's portrait is the dominant vertical subject, and an image of a driver's early car is contained in the driver's name when the card is turned horizontally.

CHAPTER 2:
COLLECTIBLES

MAXX RACE CARDS

I can't stress enough the impact that MAXX Race Cards had on the hobby of collectibles when it came on the scene in the late '80s. Along with Racing Champions and Action Performance, MAXX was one of the most influential players in the NASCAR collector market. Before these three companies got involved in the market, it seemed as though there was virtually nothing available for fans except T-shirts and hats. The company really brought a lot of innovation to the industry, such as the Legends series I created for them in 1992.

The Legends set was a group of 10 historical driver paintings scaled down to a standard baseball-card size. Drivers included Junior Johnson, Tim Richmond, Neil Bonnett, Bobby Allison, Richard Petty, Bill Elliott, Ned Jarrett, J.D. McDuffie, Rob Moroso, and popular flagman Harold Kinder.

Before I agreed to do the series, I mulled over some ideas that would really make the cards stand out because there were many, many sets on the market already, and I wanted MAXX Legends to be different. Most cards of the day were laid out in either a horizontal or vertical format, depending on the photography or artwork that was available to the production company. Even though it meant a lot of composition work on my part, I decided it would be neat for the Legends series to feature both formats on every card! The primary driver portrait and shot of the current car were laid out vertically, but on turning the card sideways, there was another image tied in with the driver's name.

The card set turned out great. Part of the set was a tribute to some of the drivers we had lost, like Richmond, McDuffie, and Moroso. For example, Moroso's card featured his Busch championship car driving through his name, and the foreground image was of the FINA car he was running on The Winston Cup circuit when he was killed in an automobile accident. There were different shots of Tim Richmond's car. There was a shot of the Wood Brothers car in which Neil Bonnett finished his career along with the Ramoc race car he had achieved some success in a few years prior.

Bill Elliott, who was driving for Junior Johnson at the time and was a spokesperson for MAXX, had a couple of different views on his card of his Budweiser car. There was some crossover in the collection when I did Junior Johnson's card, which prominently featured his own No. 3 Holly Farms Winston Cup car, plus his stable of cars for drivers Bill Elliott and Sterling Marlin.

That set of cards also represents one of my earliest opportunities for self-promotion. MAXX ran a

nice cover card showing a picture of me as part of the set, and I have to say that's when I noticed an increase in recognition by fans on the circuit. I had been at my full-time job as a NASCAR artist for five years when that set came out in 1992. Immediately I began receiving cards in the mail to autograph, and people asked me when I met them in person to sign that card. I still receive them every now and then.

Also in the early '90s I designed a display package, foil wrap, and other point-of-purchase materials for a series of racing cards MAXX was marketing. The deadline for my work happened to be exactly when Denise and I were scheduled to take part in a Rusty Wallace fan cruise sponsored by Miller Brewing. I had been invited to sign autographs and hang out with race fans because of my design work for Miller.

Most people remember a Caribbean cruise for its relaxing days and evenings spent watching the island-dotted sea drift by. Yet my most vivid memory is of the three nights I spent in my cabin painting. Normal cruise-goers take leisurely strolls and enjoy shopping sprees when the ship docks at tropical locations. I did a fast jog across the island of St. Martin to locate a FedEx box so I could get my illustrations back to MAXX on time. Needless to say, my Caribbean island experience was different from most.

MAXX also did a beautiful foil collector's set of my work for its fan club members, and I created the official Club MAXX logo.

PRESS PASS

Press Pass was another collector card company I did a few series with. One of the first sets I created for them was called Top Flight, where I did portrait illustrations for six of their drivers who had a strong jet fighter pilot look. The drivers were depicted in their full-face helmets (except for Dale Earnhardt, of course, who wore his trademark open-face helmet) as if ready to be strapped into cockpits and sent into a dogfight—hence the name Top Flight.

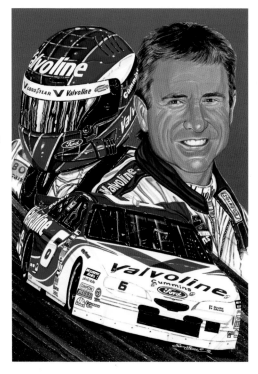

I took a medieval approach to my design of the Knights of Thunder series for Press Pass. The basis for that set was a really dramatic shot of the car in the foreground and an image of the driver suited up with helmet on in a full body pose standing behind the car, like a knight with his horse. In the night sky were the driver's number and bolts of lightning.

Knights Of Thunder proved very successful, both as a card set and later as a series of posters. In fact, it is probably my most successful poster issue to date.

Toward the end of 2002, Press Pass released an Earnhardt series using some of my favorite illustrations of him.

Mark Martin was one of six drivers featured in the Top Flight series produced for Press Pass. The series name was inspired by the jet fighter pilot–style full-face helmets featured in the drivers' portraits.

SCOREBOARD'S REMARQUE SERIES

The most work I've ever put into a run of collector cards has to be the Sam Bass Remarque series released by Scoreboard in the late '90s. It was such an innovative idea for me to create remarques—small individual sketches—for a limited number of canvas-backed cards to be inserted randomly into the collector packs.

The cards featuring 10 of my paintings were printed on a special canvas card with information on the back about the painting, some of the elements that went into it, and the creation date. On the front of the card was an area with some canvas showing through where I signed my autograph on 1,000 of them.

On 100 cards, I drew a small, individualized picture in black and white, depending on which painting was depicted. For example, the Rusty Wallace 25th anniversary painting that showed off the car design I had created for him would receive a remarque of the Miller eagle. On the Dale Earnhardt card, which was represented by "Fade To Black!" I did a small helmet remarque similar to what I had done on the full-size print of that image.

It was a massive undertaking to sign and remarque 1,100 baseball cards, but I'm told it is one of the most sought-after autographed collector series in NASCAR.

Knights of Thunder was another Press Pass card series that took its name from the pose of the helmeted driver, who was portrayed as medieval knight with his car playing the role of his horse.

KRAFT TINS

I've always enjoyed the commercial aspect of marketing projects I've been involved in with Maxwell House, Country Time Lemonade, Kellogg's Corn Flakes, Frosted Mini Wheats, and General Mills products. It's always exciting to see my work on grocery store shelves, particularly when the product is intended to be a keepsake, like the Kraft collectible tin series I created in 2003.

Cereal boxes are a great way to get my artwork out in front of fans, but there's a special thrill that comes from seeing it adorn a more durable, single-purpose product that people can save and reuse or put on a shelf with their diecast car collection. Those Kraft tins came in a series of four, each featuring one of Jack Roush's drivers and their cars. They were part of a promotion for the company's Velveeta Cheese brand.

I like working with companies willing to take nontraditional approaches to marketing their NASCAR sponsorship, because such opportunities open the door for me to show my art to a world that exists outside my gallery. I produced limited edition prints and posters of the paintings I created for the Kraft tins. Jeff Burton and I appeared at a local Food Lion grocery store and signed autographs just after the promotion started—many fans had the new tins with them.

DALE EARNHARDT TIN SERIES

In 2000, working with the Hamilton Collection, I released a series of Dale Earnhardt commemorative tins featuring four of my classic paintings, each with matching 1:64-scale collectible race cars. Unlike the Kraft tins, these were not marketing giveaways—they were sold directly to collectors.

"Hooked Up!" shows Dale in the Bass Pro Shops Monte Carlo he drove in The Winston in 1998. Dale Earnhardt and Dale Earnhardt Jr. are together in "Rising Son!," which depicts both drivers and their respective No. 3 Chevrolets from Winston Cup and Busch on the track with the sun coming up over the safety wall. "Blast From The Past!" was created to commemorate Dale's ride in The Winston in 1999, the race where The Intimidator switched back to his old yellow-and-blue Wrangler paint scheme. Finally, Dale and Taz team up in "Hot Property!" for the 2000 Daytona 500.

"Hooked Up!," which depicts Dale Earnhardt's Bass Pro Shops–sponsored car, was one of four Earnhardt paintings to be featured on collectors' tins by the Hamilton Collection. Each tin was accompanied by a matching diecast car.
Top left: The Matt Kenseth tin produced for the same collection.

COLLECTOR GUITARS

There was a time in my early life when my love of music might have eclipsed my passion for art. When I got my first guitar at the age of eight, I was crazy about the idea that I could make my own music.

Country music was the soundtrack to my childhood. My mother constantly listened to it and took me to concerts when I got older, so I've seen practically every country performer who ever toured. By the time I got to high school and discovered rock and roll (especially The Eagles and KISS) and other forms of music, I was playing in a band. In fact, it comes as a surprise to many people when they learn that I put myself through college and bought my first car with the money that I made in that band.

Just the shape and feel of an acoustic or electric guitar makes me feel like I'm holding a piece of art, and I've assembled quite a collection of them, some of which are on display in my gallery.

In 1998, as part of NASCAR's 50th anniversary celebration, musicians Kix Brooks and Ronnie Dunn called and asked me to design a one-of-a-kind guitar they wanted to present to Dale Earnhardt during a broadcast television special they were appearing in. I had been a big fan of theirs for several years and had designed their Legends race cars. Getting such a special request from Brooks & Dunn was an honor.

I worked with Gibson, one of the most famous producers of electric guitars in the world, and created a design around some drawings of Dale. Brooks & Dunn presented it to Dale, and you could tell he was quite proud to receive it.

This association with Gibson kick-started a project we had been talking about doing for a short time—a limited edition run of collectible guitars with driver themes. When I approached Dale about it, he asked, "Do you really think people are going to buy these guitars?" Even though they would retail for more than $3,000 apiece, I told him that fan response to the one Kix and Ronnie presented him had been tremendous. He agreed to let me run with the project, so I unveiled the first guitar (of a planned series of three) in February 1999. Of the 333 produced, Dale received the very first

Left: "Hot Property!" was the fourth tin in the Hamilton Collection series. It features the Taz paint scheme that Dale Earnhardt's car used in the 2000 Daytona 500. Right: The silver Intimidator edition Dale Earnhardt guitar was the second style produced in a planned series of three. The racing theme is carried out with a Simpson seat belt that serves as a strap, attached to the body of the guitar by hood pins.

one off the line, and kept it on display at his Dale Earnhardt Inc. office. The Gibson folks did a great job on that project, and the guitars are prized collectibles today.

The second guitar I did was a silver Dale edition, and the third model is still on hold. I'm not sure if it will ever see production or not.

Because the first two enjoyed such success, I got permission to produce a Dale Earnhardt Jr. Budweiser model. Dale Jr. was pleased with how it came out, because at Christmas he had me send him six of his guitars, which he gave as presents to friends in various bands he enjoyed listening to and hanging out with. It was cool to know he was proud of my efforts.

It is so appropriate that I have a strong working relationship with Gibson because I am a huge customer and fan of theirs. My personal guitar collection numbers over one hundred and many of them are classic Gibson models.

In 2002 Gibson and I became involved in a long-term, ongoing project with Nashville Superspeedway that I've been really excited about. Because both the track and Gibson Headquarters are located in Music City USA, the Nashville track has traditionally given a plain Gibson Les Paul as a race trophy. Looking for a way to make this unique reward even more special, Don Pitts from Gibson and some folks from the track asked me to design and paint a different guitar for each of its four annual events (two Busch races, one Indy Racing League, and one Craftsman Truck).

Scott Riggs won the first trophy guitar, which featured a stock car and the Nashville skyline, after the Pepsi 300 Busch race. We also gave one to NASCAR president Mike Helton, who was thrilled with it.

Now that the door has opened for my custom guitar work, I'm always looking for an opportunity to create a new Gibson design. My latest collaboration with them as of this writing is a Richard Petty "The King" commemorative guitar, decked out in Petty Blue.

Above: Sam poses with Dale Earnhardt and Dale Earnhardt Jr. after presenting them each with their guitar. (Harold Hinson)
Opposite: After the popularity of the two Dale Earnhardt guitars (the original black edition is on the left), a Dale Jr. guitar was the natural next subject, especially given Junior's enthusiasm for music.

CHAPTER 3 :
DALE EARNHARDT

I met Dale Earnhardt in the early '80s when he was driving the Wrangler car for Richard Childress. A representative from his sponsor wanted to purchase a painting I had done of Dale and the Wrangler car. I wanted to sell them the original for what seemed like a huge sum of money ($300 bought a lot of art supplies back then) but only if I knew that Dale liked the painting.

I was also concerned about what a fair arrangement might be between me and Dale concerning royalties—a situation I had no practical experience with at the time but would come to know well within a few years.

I found Dale and his wife Teresa parked in the infield of Richmond Fairgrounds Raceway, looking quite comfortable in their blue Chevrolet Blazer, and I bravely tapped on the driver's side window. Down went the glass, and I introduced myself to one of the best race car drivers the world has ever known.

"Your sponsor wants to buy this painting from me," I said, knowing that my voice was probably betraying my nervousness. "Do you like it? And how much do I need to give you if it's okay to sell it to them?" Dale smiled that mischievous grin of his, probably making a mental note to get his truck windows limo-tinted soon, and said, "Let's see it."

For the first of many times in my life, I realized at that moment I had done something that made Dale proud and I was bursting with excitement. That encounter at Richmond began a nearly 20-year working relationship and friendship wherein all our business transactions were guaranteed by a handshake and a gentleman's agreement. I always knew where I stood with him, and he knew I would never violate his trust in me. As I often told him, "I only want to make you proud of what I paint and design for you— that's what I work for."

Despite the mutual respect, taking a painting that had hour after hour of my time in it to Dale for approval was the very definition of intimidation. Fortunately, I just about always got that sly grin and a "you did good" look.

Because it was his nature to challenge himself on the track, he always loved to push those around him to a higher level of performance. One day at 7 a.m. I got a call from Dale asking if I could put together some car number designs for him to take a look at. He was on his way to a meeting, but said he would stop by my studio at 8—one hour from that moment!

The "do not disturb" sign went on the door, and my pencil blurred as I drew up a total of 85 different ideas to show him, knowing that with each new sheet of drawing paper Dale was that much closer to dropping in. When he arrived, confronted with a stack of choices, Dale paused, slid his sunglasses down his nose, smiled, and joked: "I gave you almost an hour. Is this all you got?"

In addition to all of his racing design work, Dale would ask me to handle personal and family projects, such as the paint scheme for his and Teresa's Newell motorcoach. Teresa and I collaborated on a new look for one of their jets. When Dale and Richard Petty became partners in their "7 & 7" promotion, I was asked to design the corporate logo. When the kids Kerry, Kelley, and Dale Jr. went Late Model racing, I designed their paint schemes as well.

One of the most special requests from the Earnhardt family had nothing to do with racing at all. Before Christmas of 2000, Dale's daughter Kelley asked me to do a drawing of his children and grandchildren—seven of them in all. Kelley gave me a photo from Christmas morning of Dale and Teresa opening their gift and smiling; it's a snapshot I will always cherish, knowing that the family portrait was the last piece of artwork I created for Dale.

The influence Dale had on my career and my life has been profound, and to this day I continue to benefit from his generosity. For example, the property my new gallery and studio sit on, across from Lowe's Motor Speedway, became mine after Dale and co-owner Jeff Gordon told their real estate agency to let me buy a two-acre corner parcel instead of keeping it restricted to an eight-acre lot. Dale and Jeff could have made a lot more money holding out for a giant hotel or race-related corporation to buy one big chunk of land, but instead they allowed me to grow my small business. In Daytona in 2001, Steve Park told me how proud Dale was of the role he had played in my career and securing the property for me to build my gallery on.

Dale's passing was a tremendous loss for his family, friends, fans, and the sport of racing in general. It also left a large hole in my life that will never be filled.

"Earnhardt '88"

22" x 28", 1988

In 1988 United Cerebral Palsy commissioned a painting to honor Dale at an October fundraising dinner in Charlotte.

My workload was much lighter then than it is now, so I finished "Earnhardt '88" well ahead of schedule (around September) and anxiously took it to the Richmond race to see if it met Dale's high standards. Like a lot of my character studies, there were several elements blended into the illustration, including a driver portrait, representation of a pit stop, and a strong running shot of the Goodwrench car.

At the time, after two well-received limited edition reproductions from original works, I was slowly catching on that there was a market for collectible prints. I determined my latest work would be an ideal third entry in my fledgling company's lineup, but I needed Dale's approval to proceed.

As agreed, we met at the infield media center, a very small room that was packed that weekend, where

Dale characteristically gave me a good-natured hard time before letting me off the hook.
"Does this look like me?" he asked the members of the press. "Should we let him print this?" Even before the assembled writers gave me the thumbs-up, I could see Dale liked what I had done with his image. I was on my way to releasing my first Earnhardt print.

At the UCP dinner, Dale and Teresa were complimentary of the original painting, and I was astounded to see its bidding price during the auction rise to a final $7,500. Joe Mattioli, the owner of Pocono Raceway, bought "Earnhardt '88," and I produced a run of 250 limited edition prints.

"The Wild Side"
16" x 38", 1994

It was probably the third installment of The Winston in 1987 that gave the non-points, all-star race its reputation as a free-for-all street fight.

With seven laps to go in the last of its three-segment format, Dale Earnhardt and Bill Elliott made it clear that neither would give an inch to the other on the track. Elliott had won the first and second segments but was running slightly behind Earnhardt as the two approached Charlotte Motor Speedway's front stretch after swapping paint through Turns 3 and 4. The front of Elliott's Ford nudged Earnhardt's Chevrolet, sending the Wrangler car into the grass at more than 180 miles per hour.

Although it was over in the blink of an eye, Earnhardt demonstrated the superhuman skill and coordination that would eventually lead him to seven Winston Cup championships by guiding his Chevrolet back to pavement without losing a position.

Contrary to the popular rhyming name that was immediately attached to the incident, it was technically not a "pass" in the grass, as Earnhardt was already leading Elliott when he went off-road. It was simply one of the most exciting moments in the history of stock car racing—a moment made all the sweeter when Earnhardt took the checkered flag just a few minutes later.

In 1994 Humpy Wheeler called me to his office to talk about artwork he wanted for a special infield package commemorative ticket design. "We sold 60,000 tickets for The Winston in '87," he told me, "but because of Earnhardt's stunt, I think about a million people have claimed they were there and saw it in person."

Humpy wanted me to create an image commemorating the famous drive through the infield for the front of the ticket. Sounded easy, but there was just one catch: He wanted it from the perspective of a groundhog just poking his head out of the grass right as the event was taking place.

Since I had been designing race car paint schemes for several years, I had no problem creating the "gopher-eye" angle, but drawing the background from such a low perspective was a real head-scratcher. I eventually took my camera over to the infield and took several pictures lying on the grass looking up at the grandstands. Since I did this during the driving school's lunch break, diners in The Speedway Club were probably getting a laugh out of my photo shoot, as they looked at me from above.

The commemorative ticket was very popular, and I released a print of the painting a few months later.

"Fade To Black!"

16" x 32", 1994

Fade To Black! was created to commemorate Dale's win of the 1993 Coca-Cola 600 at Lowe's Motor Speedway. As was tradition at the time, Unocal sponsored a dinner at The Speedway Club every May to honor the defending 600 champion, and I was commissioned to paint an original piece to be presented to the man of the hour.

Dale's strong personality was an ideal subject for me to portray, and I set a goal for myself to create a character study that truly did justice to his mystique. Because he had forever established himself as "The Intimidator" and "The Man in Black" to his legions of fans, I wanted to see just how much intimidation and darkness I could capture on canvas.

Placing a black car on a black background would not make a strong enough impact, so I started with a textured rich purple at the base of the stretched rectangle and gradually moved up through dark blue, and finished with a solid black sky.

The primary image of Dale with his car is one of satisfied confidence—perhaps the most intimidating attitude a driver can convey to his competition. With his tall frame, arms crossed in a relaxed manner, he leans against the No. 3 Goodwrench Chevrolet's passenger side quarter panel. His mirrored sunglasses don't let through a hint of emotion.

A smaller, secondary image of a perfectly executed pit stop just beyond Dale's left shoulder suggests his mind is already in race mode.

To this day, I'm surprised when people viewing "Fade To Black!" suddenly discover the third Earnhardt—the one that really dominates the painting once you recognize it. A subtle head-on portrait of Dale in his open-face helmet and racing goggles stares down the onlooker out of the black sky, an effect achieved with some highlights and very subtle shading.

One thing I'll always remember about that painting is that it unintentionally gave me a reason to visit Dale at his farm. I had worked on the painting until minutes before it was due at the Unocal dinner, so there was no opportunity to have it photographed for prints. After Dale and Teresa accepted it from the presenter, I asked if I could borrow the painting and was told I could stop by their farm to pick it up for photography.

After the frenzy of the Charlotte race weeks had passed, I met up with Dale at his little farmhouse office. We got into his pickup and rode through the property, with him pointing out deer and other wildlife as we made our way through paths and roads cut from the woods. It was like riding through a nature preserve to get to his house from where we had started.

Once "Fade To Black!" was in the truck, we headed back but stopped at a pond first.

"Watch this," he said. He pulled a bucket from his truck and shook it, which made the water stir with more fish than I could ever imagine the pond holding. He threw the feed in the water and pulled a fishing pole out of the truck. As soon as the line hit the surface, something big took the bait and Dale handed me the pole. "With a name like Bass, you ought to be able to handle this."

It was just the coolest thing! I don't really fish, but Earnhardt had hooked a fish and let me reel it in. To this day, it's the biggest fish I've ever caught. It was something he seemed to take great delight in.

I think "Fade To Black!" was a favorite of Dale's, too, because it captured the mystique of his personality. I could tell he liked the title quite a bit. Later that year, he did a commercial bumper for ESPN's coverage of one of the races, where he was in the TV truck as if he were producing the live broadcast. The spot showed a racing action scene and then cut to Dale, who would give the direction to "fade to black." The screen would go black; the next scene would come up, and he would say it again.

Fade to black...

"360°!"
22" x 26", 1994

It's not often I get asked by a driver to create a painting for a second-place finish, but that's what happened after the Sept. 25, 1994, race at Martinsville.

Kenny Wallace, substituting for Ernie Irvan, tangled with Dale at top speed on the 34th lap of the Goody's 500. Instead of hitting the wall or spinning into the infield, Dale managed to stand on the gas and steer through a 360-degree controlled loop losing only a single position. Normally, a driver backs up about 30 spots when he spins at Martinsville.

It was an amazing bit of driving that was his way of saying, "I'm after my seventh championship and nothing's going to stop me."

For nearly 40 laps Dale and Rusty Wallace banged sheet metal and fought each other for the lead like heavyweight prizefighters refusing to drop. With three laps to go, Dale's brakes overheated, leaving Rusty to take the win.

Dale called me on his way home that evening, clearly still excited about his wild ride from early in the race. "We've got to do a painting of that!" he told me. I was glad to get this news because I always tried to come up with something special for Dale's Christmas present, and his suggestion filled the bill for that year perfectly.

I created "360°!" with a circular theme. The way the title was printed, it was a big number 3—synonymous with his car—then the 60, then the degree symbol. The main picture of Dale coming out of the spin and righting himself was the focal point of the circle. Inside the circle were three other shots of the spin, from his getting tapped in the rear to his being backward. You see a little bit of the front bumper of Kenny's car; everything in there told a story.

The action moves in a counterclockwise motion, the same way the cars drive on the track. On the original painting and 36 artist's proofs, I installed a clock mechanism that ran counterclockwise with an overhead shot of his car spinning backward. It took a lot of effort to find a supplier for such a mechanism.

When I gave Dale the original—which was much larger than the prints—the week before Christmas, the first thing he said when he saw it was, "Look at that car moving!" I could tell he enjoyed having an outside view of his spin.

"Dale Earnhardt Appreciation Day"

23" x 18", 1994

About two weeks before Dale was honored as a "favorite son" during the Kannapolis Appreciation Day in 1994, event organizers asked me to create a painting depicting the driver's ties to his hometown.

Considering that the day caught national attention and that Kannapolis is not a big city, the celebration all but shut the place down. It was a huge event, with country-music performers Brooks & Dunn taking center stage.

The painting "Kannapolis Appreciation Day" is one of those projects I enjoyed doing because I got to use a lot of nonrace images. The Cannon Mills factory, tourism bureau building, Gem Theater, and war memorial—all scenes of life around downtown Kannapolis—appeared in my painting along with a checkered flag, the official city seal, a perfectly blue sky and, of course, Dale himself standing in the foreground with arms folded. His No. 3 Chevrolet was parked on the grounds of Cannon Mills. Thousands of posters were produced from the painting so everyone there would have a memento of the day.

It was a very special day for Dale, surrounded by the people he had grown up with and who had meant a lot to him, and it was my great fortune to present him with his painting on stage. That night at the country club was a celebrity roast–style dinner in his honor.

Dale hung the painting in his Busch shop, where I later saw it displayed amid a group of mounted deer heads. I knew then that he considered it a special piece because he was enormously proud of his game trophies, and the Busch shop was like a sanctuary to him, an escape during the week where he could just be one of the guys.

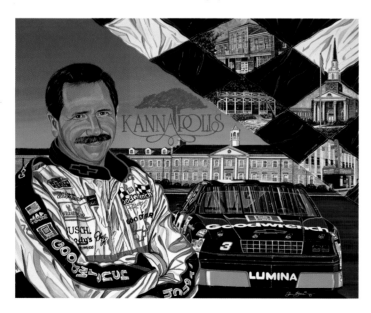

"The Magnificent Seven!"

25" x 27", 1994

My favorite toys when I was growing up were cap pistols, cowboy hats, and my Lone Ranger mask. I've never had it verified, but I may be a distant relative of the outlaw Sam Bass, a bank robber who died on his 27th birthday in 1878 after a gun battle with Texas rangers. That genetic link might explain my love of the deserts of the southwest and all their unique colors and shapes.

A lot of my paintings draw from the legends of the Wild American West—a time of gunslingers, horses, and showdowns in the street—because I see a lot of analogies between race car drivers and the outlaws of old. Both groups travel a lot to find an income. Both try to leave town with as much money as they can. Both have dangerous jobs that most men prefer to avoid. Cowboys rely entirely on their horses; a racer's livelihood depends on horsepower. The public seldom gets to know either group up close and personal, instead creating legends around a few memorable documented acts like a stage-coach robbery or a Daytona 500 win.

I've always loved John Wayne, and I think it's safe to say that Dale Earnhardt was the "Duke" of NASCAR, with his all-American, take-no-prisoners approach and larger-than-life stature. He was the perfect subject for my first painting with a Western motif.

When Dale locked up his seventh Winston Cup championship at Rockingham in 1994 with two races left to go in the season, I was asked to commemorate the occasion in paint by the producers of a post-race ESPN television show called "NASCAR Shop Talk."

Time was short, so I got to work immediately. I knew what elements I wanted to incorporate into my painting—Dale, his seven championship cars, and the trophy—but my inspiration for the piece actually came by way of a Japanese film I had seen in college: The Seven Samurai. This 1954 classic from director Akira Kurosawa told the story of a small village that recruits seven warriors to defend it against an invading army. It was so popular that John Sturges remade it six years later as The Magnificent Seven and transplanted the endangered village to Mexico. Steve McQueen and Yul Brynner play two of the seven gunslingers hired as the community's bodyguards.

The Magnificent Seven was, in my mind, one of the greatest westerns ever, and I wanted to forever link Earnhardt's record-tying seventh championship to the cool, methodical way the movie's heroes dispatched the banditos with courage, cleverness, and commitment. To my way of thinking, the seven championship cars were Dale's banditos.

Just researching the details for each car took a great deal of time, especially the decals and subtle body changes on the Goodwrench cars. The image of Dale walking toward the foreground was based on a photograph I took of him on pit road as he was headed for a prerace driver introduction. I placed the trophy so it looked as if it were rising up out of the desert landscape.

At 7:30 on the morning we would be taping the show at Richard Childress Racing, I was still framing the piece; I barely made it to the shop by my 9 a.m. deadline. Dale came in a little bit before his appointed time of 1 p.m. and immediately asked me, "What ya got, Bass?" I handed him "The Magnificent

Seven!" and was relieved when he got that big Earnhardt grin on his face.

Even though we sold a ton of those prints and it was a very successful painting, my real reward for all that work was seeing that the man who had just won his seventh Winston Cup championship was happy with something I had created.

"Quick Silver!"
32" x 25", 1995 (Opposite)

"Black Attack!"
28" x 22", 1997 (shown on page 53)

In February 1995 Fred Wagenhals of Action Performance asked me to create a painting depicting Dale's upcoming Winston ride for some special packaging needs. (Looking back on it, it's amazing how that silver select car really started the whole trend of commemorative and one-time paint jobs. Where would the diecast world be today if not for that?)

Action wanted to unveil the car on the Tuesday before the Saturday night race, and there was a shroud of secrecy over the whole project. Fred's idea worked, because the public went crazy for the new car and bought a lot of Action's diecast models.

In the meantime, I had done another painting of the car to give to Dale, and I presented it to him in the Charlotte media center after the unveiling. As with most of my work, I created a series of limited edition prints—500 in this case—with 50 artist's proofs to sell through the gallery. Special silver ink was used to make the prints, and I was really pleased when I saw the finished sheets.

Dale had agreed to autograph copies of "Quick Silver!", so it was with great enthusiasm that I took a box of them out to his farm for a signing session. I remember it was hotter than heck and that Dale amused himself by signing each print faster than I could get the next off the table to put in front of him.

It was a really fun couple of hours for me, even though I was getting a workout as I tried to keep up with Dale. During our high-speed game, he told me how much he liked the painting but that he would really like to see the black-and-silver treatment performed on the black Goodwrench car he always drove.

Because of other commitments and projects, it was almost two years later before I completed the artwork "Black Attack!"—the fulfillment of Dale's request. I couldn't wait to show it to him, so I took it with me to Daytona and visited Dale in his motorcoach one day after practice.

Before I unveiled it, he asked, "Am I going to like this?" I told him, "I hope so. I think the portrait shots are better than in 'Quick Silver!' but it features the black car."

I unveiled it. He looked at it and said, "I don't like it." Of all the low points an artist can have, that had to be the lowest in my career! I thought I had nailed it.

I asked him what he didn't like about it. "I wanted it done entirely in black and silver," he explained. "I like what you did in that first painting." He wanted it without the blue in the Goodwrench logo and other splashes of color—solid black interrupted only by silver lines. I was crushed to think it didn't meet his approval, but then he surprised me.

"How many prints are you going to make of this?"

"Well, none, I guess."

"It's a great painting," he assured me. "It's just not what I had wanted, but my fans will love it."

Dale was a person who always knew what he wanted, and I realized he wasn't trying to hurt my feelings. So I accepted his compliment and decided to get it right for next time.

The painting moved to the back burner again as other projects monopolized my workdays, but I managed to finish it the week of the fall Charlotte races. Dale used to have an open house every year at his Chevrolet dealership in Newton, N.C., for fans to stop by and visit. It was his way of thanking them for their support throughout his career, and the event always drew a giant crowd. I had my own tradition with the open house as well; each year I tried to have a new painting to present to Dale to show my appreciation for his business and friendship.

At the end of the day, I stood in line with the rest of the fans and marveled at the number of people waiting patiently to meet their racing hero. It seems everybody has a brother or uncle who claims Dale "snubbed" him on an autograph request; usually these are people who caught him on his way to a drivers' meeting or press conference. Knowing that Dale's day at the dealership normally kept him chairbound for 14 straight hours reminded me that The Intimidator never intentionally snubbed any fan.

I knew I could have interrupted Dale long enough to give him the painting, but I wasn't about to break in front of a family whose entire day had been scheduled around this event. As I shuffled my way closer to the front, a representative from General Motors stood up and announced the company was presenting Dale with the Corvette sitting in the showroom. I remember the car was one of the first built that year. I think it was the second or third off the assembly line; in other words, it was any collector's dream.

Dale seemed extremely happy to accept the gift and got right back to his fans. As for me? I was selfishly thinking, "That's just great! I'll give him a painting just minutes after he's been handed the keys to a $50,000 Corvette!"

Now remember, this is my second try at getting this painting right, so I had to get up my courage when there was nobody left between me and Dale. When I handed him the painting he looked it over, then stood up without saying anything and set the painting in the Corvette's luggage space. He walked back over to the table, sat down, looked at me and said, "Now that car is really special to me."

This story, to me, is a great summary of the relationship Dale and I had. He knew how hard I had worked on that piece. He had just gotten a free, really awesome Corvette, but he let me know that my effort was just as special to him.

In the course of my career, I'm sure I'll do many more paintings of Dale, but there will never again be that reward of showing him something new and getting his approval for it. It was always the most

intimidating experience to show him something, but the reward for getting it right was worth it.

Because the creation of that painting took place over a couple of years and took me through a rollercoaster of emotions as an artist, it will always be one of my favorite Dale Earnhardt paintings. It sums up Dale and what he meant to me—a "tough as nails" exterior to many, and a heart of gold underneath—something that most people never got to see.

I miss the relationship we had, because it really challenged me to do my best. Whether it was the slant of his car's number or the design of the car, coach, or airplane, trying to please him made me a better artist. It is that personal challenge I miss now that he's gone.

"Blaze Of Glory!"

24" x 27", 1996

One of my very special memories of Dale, one of the chances I had to do something for him, was in 1996 when he ran a one-time Olympic paint scheme in The Winston.

I was working on a painting depicting Dale and the new car called "Blaze Of Glory!" but hit a speed bump when it came to an area showing him inside the car, because his standard helmet didn't exactly complement the car's paint scheme from an artistic standpoint. Dale had been adamant about not changing helmet or uniform designs through most of his career. He usually stuck to the Darth Vader-ish solid black, but there was a time when his Goodwrench helmet sported red and white in addition to black. There were also many years early in his career where he wore a plain out-of-the-box white one.

I took some liberties with the painting and designed a matching stars and stripes helmet for Dale, which Simpson reproduced in a small collector's version. My greatest thrill, though, came when Dale actually wore the helmet design in The Winston.

The president of the Olympic committee was present when the car was originally unveiled in Atlanta, and I had the great fortune to ride with him and Dale around the track. In one of his typically generous gestures, Dale took it upon himself to tell his guest great things about me and my artwork. I was blown away to be present when the most famous driver in NASCAR was recommending my work to the head of the most prestigious sporting event in the world.

I wound up getting a letter from the committee after the painting debuted congratulating me on my participation. It was a very special project for me.

"Ready To Rumble!"

30" x 22", 1996

One of my favorite illustrations of Dale is "Ready To Rumble!," which I painted for Bristol Motor Speedway to use on the Food City 500 souvenir race program cover in April 1996.

I thought a great concept would be to have Earnhardt posed in a combination of recognizably macho scenarios: the high school showoff who has the fastest car and knows it; the forfit neighborhood tough guy who owns a street corner and wants everybody else to know it; and the veteran Wild West gunslinger no one in the saloon wants to make eye contact with.

I wanted to portray Dale as having the ease of confidence and certainty about his place on the track. For this painting, I saw him as being ready to go, ready to race anybody at any time, taking on all comers.

The idea started with putting him in an early morning sunrise setting in front of a brick wall sprayed with graffiti. He's leaning against his car in his leather jacket and sunglasses as if to say, "I'm The Intimidator. Let's go."

The painting got a tremendously positive reaction from Dale, and his fans just love it. Thanks to the magic of the drawing table, there are people who to this day think I managed to get Dale to pose in front of a brick wall in the infield of Bristol. Actually, it was a series of photos that a few photographers and I took. They just blended inside my head to create that one scene. I'm not even sure you could find a wall like that anywhere near the speedway.

"Ready To Rumble!" is 100 percent pure attitude. It's Earnhardt in all his glory: that iconic lean against his car with his arms folded, and the leather jacket nobody could wear quite like Dale that gave him a look of someone you didn't want to mess with.

Psyching out the competition plays a big part in racing, probably in equal proportion to luck, coordination, and skill. The projection of confidence was a science Dale Earnhardt raised to an art form throughout his career.

This is definitely one of my favorite paintings. It is so much so, in fact, that I used virtually the same composition in 2003's "Tradin' Paint!" featuring Dale Jr.

"Champion's Choice!"

24" x 27", 1997

Champion's Choice!" is like one of those box-within-a-box-within-a-box things you see sometimes in specialty gift shops: It's a painting I created, depicting a cereal box I illustrated, showing a race car I designed.

In 1997 General Mills gave me the chance to design a special Wheaties paint scheme for Dale to run in The Winston that year. I dressed up the Goodwrench Chevy with a Wheaties orange base and white bottom with blue outline and accents.

While drawing the car, I made some renderings of what Dale's uniform and helmet would look like. I combined car and driver in a single illustration the folks at General Mills liked so much that they asked to use it as part of a special series of Wheaties boxes.

That was definitely a career highlight for me because I know I'll never be on the front of a Wheaties box, but it answered forever the question of whether drivers should be considered athletes. The things Dale did on the track and the way he was able to handle his car through impossible situations demonstrated that he had the physical agility, hand-eye coordination, and stamina of a world-class athlete—the Wheaties box just acknowledged the fact to the world.

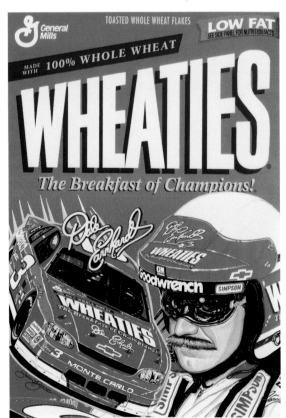

It meant a lot to Dale that he was chosen to be the first race car driver on a box of Wheaties. I could see how honored he was during the press announcement in Atlanta where he and Richard Childress unveiled an eight-foot-tall cereal box featuring my artwork.

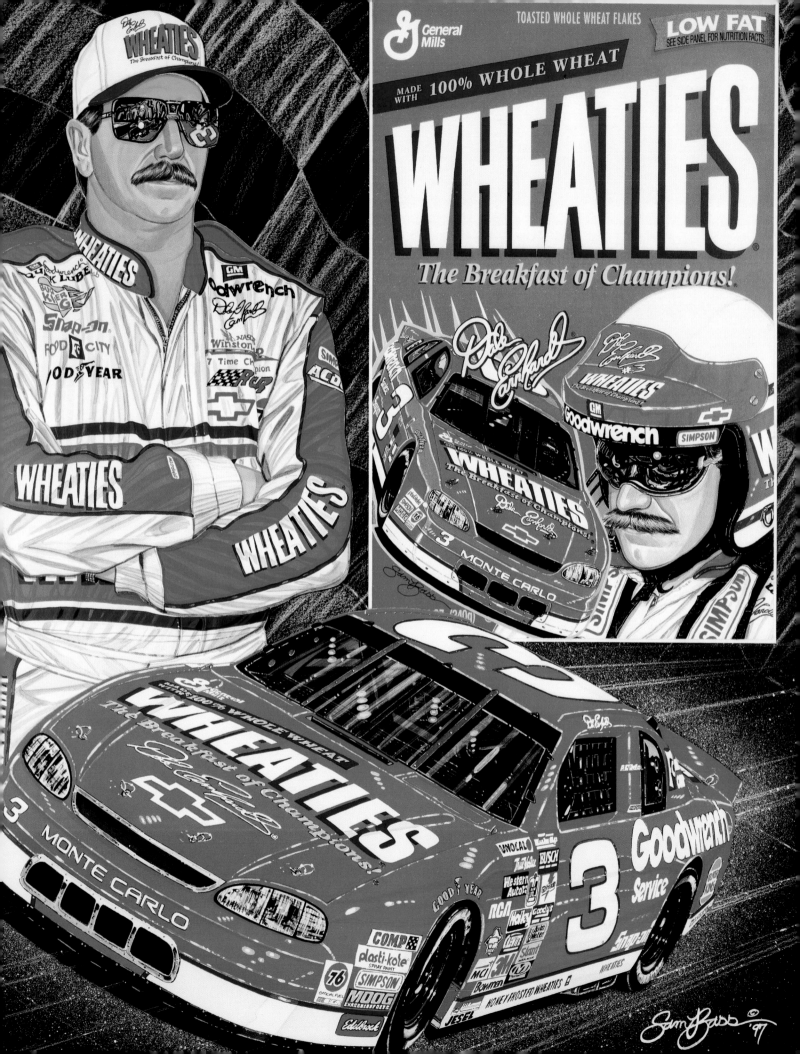

"Finally, First!"

34" x 27", 1998

This painting was 20 years in the making," I told Dale when I showed him "Finally, First!" toward the end of 1998. He appreciated the humor of the title, because his fans and friends had long anticipated the Daytona 500 victory commemorated in the image. That win was a highlight of Dale's career, and I made a special effort to capture the excitement behind it on canvas.

Once it became clear that Dale had the strongest car on the track and wasn't going to let anything keep him from winning, I started thinking, "How am I going to depict this in a painting?"

Because my schedule was so overloaded coming out of Daytona, I did not have a chance to begin the painting until later in the year. I started with the central image of him in victory lane on top of his car with the long-awaited trophy, then added scenes of Dale driving down pit road while members of other teams gave him high fives and shook his hand. Other elements include a driver portrait, a running shot of the car on the Daytona track, an image of Dale spinning in the grass—there's just so much going on it feels like you are at the race. There is a whole book wrapped up in this painting, which I think is why people looking at it are drawn in so completely.

Once it was done, I agonized over the title. So many different clever newspaper headlines came out after the win, but I wanted something that went along with the uniqueness of the painting. I thought the word finally should be used, because it conveyed the sense of anticipation being rewarded, and then I couldn't resist using alliteration by repeating the f sound.

I called Dale and told him I had a Christmas present for him. When he and Teresa stopped by my old gallery on speedway property, I had "Finally, First!" sitting on an easel with a drape over it, ready for unveiling. When I pulled back the cover, Dale smiled proudly. I still have a picture of him and me standing behind the painting.

As they were leaving, Dale reminded me how keenly aware he was of what went on in my business when he asked, "We're doing prints on this, aren't we?"

"I hope so," I replied. "People have been ordering them since February," I explained. Fans were expecting me to document the victory.

It was the Thursday before The Winston Cup banquet when we were having this conversation, which meant we would have to hustle to get prints out in time for Christmas. "Get them out to me so I can sign them," he said, surprising me. "I'll be back from the banquet on Monday. Can you have them ready?"

With an invitation like that, I wasted no time getting in touch with my printer, and we worked all weekend to have prints ready for Dale to sign on Monday. We set up for the marathon autograph session in a room Dale had just for that purpose. At any given time, there were usually around 25,000 items on the shelves Dale had received from fans and licensees asking for a signature. It took the Daytona winner only a couple of hours to handle my stack of limited edition prints, but I knew his effort would mean everything to the fans giving or receiving them as Christmas gifts.

By the end of that Monday, we were shipping "Finally, First!" to our customers. To this day, I consider it to be one of the best paintings of my career, and Dale's response to it only boosted my enthusiasm for it.

I would place the Daytona victory on the same level as Dale's seventh NASCAR Winston Cup championship in terms of fan excitement. Only his Talladega triumph, his final win, where he gained 18 positions in the last four laps, might be as much of a career highlight. That's a painting I still plan to do.

There are many memories, both sad and special, that I have of the period after we lost Dale in the 2001 Daytona 500. I was very touched when Ward Burton called me at the office to ask if I still had any copies of "Finally, First!" with Dale's autograph. He said that as much as he idolized The Intimidator, he had never asked him to autograph anything and wanted a signed copy of that painting to frame and give to his sons. Ward told me the painting was special to him because it had meant so much to Dale. He wanted something tangible that could pass along his memories of Dale to the next generation.

The thought that a painting of mine could transcend the sadness of the moment really meant a lot to me. It was such a special request, especially coming from a driver whose public conduct and professionalism I admire very much.

"Above The Rest!"
12" x 24", 1999

I was standing in the infield at Bristol Motor Speedway in 1999 with my camera when a perfect photo opportunity presented itself. Dale Earnhardt was standing on top of the pit wall in his famous prerace pose: arms crossed, his face displaying confidence.

Now I don't consider myself a great photographer, but I always have my camera handy at racetracks because I take a lot of reference photos of drivers, cars, pavement, and grandstands for my artwork. The half-mile bowl of Bristol has an infield that's incredibly small but perfect for catching candid snapshots of drivers.

Earnhardt was perfectly framed in the lens of my Nikon, but before I could commit the image to film, he looked away. I kept the camera at the ready, hoping to capture the look of Dale studying his competition. After a few more false starts, I realized he was aware of my attempts to play amateur photographer and was deliberately making it tough for me.

Between his comedic efforts and the interruptions we both encountered, it took me nearly two hours to get the picture I wanted. Finally, with my patience waning, I again saw the pose that had eluded me and in 1/250th of a second, my shutter burned the image onto film.

Later, in my studio, I considered how best to capture in paint the essence of Dale's personality with that one picture. I knew that two of Dale's favorite colors were black and silver, so it was an easy decision to paint him using just the two.

My most significant memory about "Above The Rest!" is that Dale's mom, Martha Earnhardt, came into the gallery shortly after I hung the painting. She looked it over and declared, "You got him!" Hearing those three words has got to rank as one of the all-time crowning achievements of my career. Everybody knows what a true fan of Dale's I was, but to have his mother tell me she was proud of what I

Preceding pages—"Blast From The Past!", 30" x 23", 1999
For the 1999 running of The Winston, Dale Earnhardt ran
the Wrangler paint scheme that he had popularized in the
mid 1980s.

captured in her son was the ultimate approval.

Martha's feelings about the painting are why the first thing a visitor to the Dale Earnhardt Tribute Center in Kannapolis encounters is a column with a 9-foot-tall reproduction of "Above The Rest!" Doing the tribute is a big project and a monumental part of my career, but I thought there could be no better way for people to enter this work in progress than for that one image that meant so much to his mom to be the first thing they see.

"Blast From The Past!"
30" x 23", 1999

I was fortunate to know Dale early in his career when he was driving for Wrangler Jeans, a sponsor whose blue-and-yellow color combination still ranks among my favorite paint schemes in the history of NASCAR. He streaked to three of his seven Winston Cup championships and took his famous wild ride through the Charlotte Motor Speedway infield grass at 180 miles per hour wearing those colors.

The walls of my gallery include quite a few paintings of Dale driving that Wrangler car for all it was worth, but my favorite depiction is something I did in 1999, several years and four championships after he began driving for Goodwrench.

"Blast From The Past!" illustrates a one-time reunion orchestrated for The Winston at Lowe's Motor Speedway that year. In an event already famous for single-use commemorative paint schemes, Richard Childress Racing's retro-Wrangler look captured the attention of the media. Many nostalgic race fans, including me, enjoyed seeing blue and yellow on Earnhardt's contemporary No. 3 Goodwrench Chevrolet Monte Carlo.

In the painting, I portrayed the "One Tough Customer" look of Dale from the mid-'80s on a Wanted poster against a Western desert scene under a night sky, with the new Wrangler Monte Carlo emerging from the darkness of a night race and a portrait of Dale in a blue and yellow uniform behind the car. Look closely and you can see a subtle image of the traditional black Goodwrench Monte Carlo in the night sky.

You never knew if Dale's uniform would match a special commemorative paint scheme or not. Since Dale chose to wear his standard white Goodwrench uniform while in the Wrangler car, this painting really is the only place you can see driver and car in matched colors.

Because he was so fond of that Goodwrench uniform, it kept the same basic layout from 1988 through 2001. In the history of NASCAR, you're unlikely to find a driver who kept the same uniform design for so many years. It really became the look that people had in their minds when they thought of Dale: that stark white uniform with the black and red bands around his chest. I had the opportunity to work on the tweaks and redesigns of that uniform through the years, but he never wanted it to stray far from the original.

When I finished "Blast From The Past!", the coolest thing was getting to deliver the first print during the weekend of The Winston. Dale was inside the track practicing and Teresa was in their condo by her-

self. I got to present the image to her, which was a real pleasure.

That painting covered a lot of years of Dale's career, from his early Wrangler days to the running of the Wrangler/Goodwrench car in The Winston, but it also bridged a vast span of time that I worked with the Earnhardts. The early Wrangler days are when I first got involved with Dale and Teresa, so "Blast From The Past!" is very much a nostalgic piece for Sam Bass the artist as well as for Sam Bass the race fan.

KANNAPOLIS INTIMIDATORS

I could have named my business Sam Bass Art or The Sam Bass Gallery, but I chose Sam Bass Illustration & Design to let people know I am more than an artist—I am a designer, as well. Over the years I've had the opportunity to create a lot of forfit logos, uniform designs, and car and transporter paint schemes.

Probably the peak of my work as a designer—the job I can always point to and say, "That's why I got into this business!"—began when I was approached in 2000 by the local Class A affiliate to the Chicago White Sox baseball team.

I was asked what I thought about changing the name of the team from Kannapolis Boll Weevils to Kannapolis Intimidators to associate the team with hometown hero Dale Earnhardt. I thought it was a great idea and would bring a lot of attention to their minor-league ball club. My initial talks with the Boll Weevil representatives were so secret that even Dale himself was not yet aware of what was going on. My involvement in that job put me at the front end of a very big deal for the town of Kannapolis.

Our first meeting dealt more with questions like: "Do you think Dale will be interested in an offer to become a part owner?" and "How comfortable do you think he'll be about having his name associated with a baseball team?" Knowing what a fan of the sport Dale was, and having seen his pride in being recognized as Kannapolis' "favorite son," I told them I thought The Intimidator would be all over the idea.

I got to work right away on some logo and design work. One of the really popular logo ideas I hit upon was the "Faceball," which incorporated a caricature of Dale's face into a baseball, complete with sunglasses and moustache. Although it was universally liked, Dale was a little self-conscious about his image being so strongly promoted ahead of the team itself.

Instead, we decided to go with another design I had created as a more subtle reference to Dale—the Intimidating K. It was basically a fierce looking capital letter K, for Kannapolis.

At a press conference in November at Lowe's Motor Speedway, I presented Dale with a painting of the Faceball and was told by several media members that they liked the caricature logo even better than the Intimidating K.

Opposite: Detail of "A Texas Size Win" shown on page 77. Right: "Follow The Line!" 2003, 21" x 27" The themes of continuity and tradition are the subject of "Follow the Line", which commemorates the years of experience passed from one racing generation to the next.

CHAPTER 4:
DALE EARNHARDT JR.

I met Dale Jr. when he was just a little kid sitting on the back of his dad's transporter in The Winston Cup garage. After that, I saw him off and on as I dealt with his father on paintings and car designs.

There's an old photograph in my collection taken at a UNOCAL pit crew contest showing Dale's Wrangler car getting serviced at top speed as officials monitor their timing equipment. I'm standing in the background crowd watching the contest, and a few feet away is Dale Jr., happily looking on. Knowing now what a gifted driver he turned out to be makes me wonder just what was going through his mind at that moment. Did he realize then how much pressure having a legend for a father would mean, especially when he shared his name? Was it an intimidating thought for him, or was he in total control just like Dale?

When Dale Jr. started racing Street Stocks at Concord Motorsport Park at the age of 17, he got off to a slow start but kept at it for two seasons until he was ready to move to Late Model Stock Cars and compete with his brother, Kerry, and sister, Kelley.

Dale asked me to create some designs for his kids' Western Steer–sponsored race cars, which I was more than happy to do. On a couple of layouts I drew their car numbers slanting toward the rear of the car instead of toward the front. When he saw those illustrations, I could tell immediately that Dale did not like the idea. "Why do you have the numbers leaning backward?" he asked.

I told him my concept was to think of the number as something attached to the car, like a radio antenna, that is blown backward by the great speed the car is traveling. Even though the number was painted on, the car was rocketing through time and space to the point that the image of the number was being warped.

"When you run, how do you run?" Dale stood up to demonstrate. "Do you run leaning forward," he mimicked a sprinter, "or backward?" he asked as he leaned back, displaying a remarkably subtle sense of physical humor. It is one of the great all-time visuals I have in my mind of Dale, and it reminded me to never take another drawing to him with the number pointing anywhere but forward.

Although I had put together some pretty radical ideas for the kids' cars, the designs were ultimately whittled down to basic colors—red, white, and black—with a stripe on the sides. "The kids are going to wreck a lot as they learn to race," Dale said. "Keep the paint jobs simple."

Dale Jr.'s Busch debut took place at Lowe's Motor Speedway in October 1997. Dale's agent, Don Hawk, pulled together the sponsorship from Wrangler, Gargoyles—several different corporations—and asked me to design the car. Dale had his annual open house at his dealership the week before the race, so I was able to present Dale Jr. with a framed copy of his car design. Unfortunately, Junior crashed the car in practice and sat out the race.

For his first full year as a Busch driver in 1998, Junior drove the AC-Delco paint scheme I had originally designed for Dale when NASCAR went to Japan. I was especially proud to see him win the Busch championship in that car—and not just one year, but two in a row!

No one was surprised—least of all me, because I had been working with Budweiser to design Junior's No. 8 Monte Carlo—at the announcement in 1999 that Dale Jr. would be driving in Winston Cup that year for DEI on a limited schedule.

Because it was such a high-profile debut, everyone involved had specific ideas about how the car should look. The Budweiser folks were set on retaining an all-red paint scheme because red, of course, is such a strong part of the company's marketing identity. Dale insisted that an element of black be incorporated because of that color's association with the Earnhardt legend. Junior's preference was that it have a strong graphic appeal and not look like he was driving a boring race car. On top of it all was DEI's request that the color scheme in some way complement the look of teammate Steve Park's Pennzoil car.

As the designer, it was my responsibility to work within all of the seemingly conflicting parameters and produce a look that made everybody happy. I got right to work, turning out ideas for the Bud car with several radical schemes.

The winning design made its debut at Lowe's Motor Speedway's Coca-Cola 600, where Junior started in eighth position and finished 16th. The earliest version had a black roof and pillars; later seasons would see the black element toned down. Junior drove the car in five more Cup races that year, finishing a best 10th place at Richmond, before starting his full-time rookie season in 2000.

Junior's success has been an amazing thing to watch because he didn't exactly set the track on fire in Late Models. Everybody expected him to be a world-class driver the first time he got behind the wheel of a car because they were so eager to see the Earnhardt name rule another generation of speedways and short tracks. What they were forgetting is that Dale, as well as every other champion, had to develop and grow as a driver. In other words, you have to learn to crawl before you can dominate.

If his name were anything other than Earnhardt, people would be amazed at the success he's had, but because he is an Earnhardt, it was almost expected. Dale Jr.'s story has only just begun. I'm very eager to see how he and the other young drivers change the face of NASCAR for this generation, just as Richard Petty and Dale Earnhardt did in their time.

"Rising Son!"

26" x 22", 1998

I created "Rising Son!" as a cover for the spring 1998 Bristol program to commemorate Junior's first year in the Busch series. Not only was the racing world enjoying Junior's entry into NASCAR, but Bristol Motor Speedway and the two Earnhardt cars were carrying associate sponsorship from Food City, who also sponsored The Winston Cup race, making the painting's theme a natural choice that would please everybody.

Coming up with the concept of comparing the younger Earnhardt to a rising sun was an easy one, because people were certain he would be achieving great things. I centered the sun in the frame, coming up over the back of the steeply banked Bristol speedway. Father and son face off in opposing portraits, while their cars compete side-by-side on the track below.

I felt the painting had a lot of impact because it was one of the first times I was able to depict father and son together in a competitive environment. The image was a sneak peek of what people were expecting for Junior's eventual move to Winston Cup.

Fans at Bristol really responded to that cover. I know because I was there watching them buy the programs, and they were blown away by the forcefulness of that image—even the ones who weren't Earnhardt fans! That enthusiasm carried over when I offered "Rising Son!" as limited edition prints and fine art posters. It was very well received.

"We Have Lift Off!"
23" x 30", 1999

In 1998 the term "D-Day" found its way back into the language of popular culture with Steven Spielberg's blockbuster hit *Saving Private Ryan*. The invasion of Normandy, France, by wave after wave of Allied troops was a major factor in the outcome of World War II, and the code word for that military movement, D-Day, has come to mean that an unstoppable force will be unleashed on a specific date.

When Dale Jr.'s inevitable Winston Cup debut was scheduled to take place during the Coca-Cola 600 at Lowe's Motor Speedway, someone in the Budweiser camp with a talent for hyperbole came up with "E-Day" to suggest the event would one day be regarded as pivotal in NASCAR history.

The announcement was made a month prior to the event, and Budweiser printed 750,000 copies of my design layout "We Have Lift Off!" to be distributed to fans and customers. The image depicts the No. 8 Budweiser car from five different angles, with the transporter in the background and Dale Jr. standing at the ready. On the bottom of the poster I placed the E-Day logo.

I was pleased that a large version of the image served as a backdrop for Junior during the press conference, flanked by two big illustrations of the car I created just for the announcement.

Five years later, Dale Jr. has become a magnet for the youthful audience NASCAR has been seeking. Young people who were once outside the world of racing have been drawn in because of Junior's cool charisma and style. He's made himself—and a lot of other drivers, by association—as hip as rap stars and basketball players. He's been featured on MTV alongside the icons of extreme sports who themselves see the drum-playing driver of No. 8 as an equal and, in some cases, an idol.

Maybe calling Dale Jr.'s debut E-Day wasn't such a stretch after all.

"Tradin' Paint!"
30" x 22", 2003 (shown on page 72-73)

The long-awaited companion piece to "Ready to Rumble!" features Dale Earnhardt Jr. in a modern version of the same setting. The seven years that separate the two images are brought together by subtle touches such as the "3" shaded in Dale Jr.'s "8" and black donut on his car, suggesting a rub from the Goodwrench car... but, in the new illustration, Dale Jr. assumes the famous pose and somehow makes it his own.

"A Texas Size Win!"
21" x 27", 2001

Dale Jr. showed the world he had the stuff of champions when he crossed the finish line at Texas Motor Speedway in 2000, his Winston Cup rookie year, to win the DIRECTV 500. It was the first Cup win for the two-time Busch champion, and his father made only a brief appearance in victory circle to congratulate him, clearly letting his son have the spotlight all to himself.

I was there and got to enjoy the celebration, all the while letting the artistic side of my brain soak up details and impressions for what I knew would be a powerful painting. Because Junior's first Busch win had also been on the Texas track, the moment was all the sweeter. Confetti and fireworks flew, and the members of the Budweiser crew were out of their minds with happiness.

The bear hug between father and son was such an emotional sight for everyone in victory lane. I remember at that moment noticing that Dale's smile was so deep—not his usual mischievous grin—that his eyes were almost closed from the effort. For those few seconds in victory lane, Dale was not an intimidating legend but a proud father, and everybody got a quick glimpse of Dale the man.

Dale didn't show a lot of emotion, whether in public or private, but he had his subtle ways of communicating his friendship and when he was happy. One of his favorite ways to say hello, especially if you didn't see him coming, was a pinch on the shoulder or a good-natured punch in the arm. I'm not frail by any means, but I think a few of his greetings over the years came close to ending my painting career.

As is often the case with a really hot topic like Junior's first win, my customers were already calling to put themselves on a waiting list for a painting they knew would someday be offered as a print. Even DEI wanted to know when a painting would be made of the moment.

Unfortunately, my prescheduled workload kept me from getting to that painting all through 2000 and into 2001. When Dale was killed in February 2001, the tremendous personal loss I felt made me reprioritize the work I was doing in order to finish jobs that would give some comfort to his family and fans. At the top of my list was a painting of the Texas win, which Texas track President Eddie Gossage and I decided would be a very appropriate program cover for his track's upcoming race, as it would mark the event's anniversary.

"A Texas Size Win!" was done with a heavy heart, but I knew Dale would want me to do the painting. Remembering how quickly Dale had vacated Junior's victory lane made me realize he would want the painting to focus on his son, so I rendered the hug using a transparent technique. Junior's hat is askew on his head, showing the force of the celebratory embrace, and I recalled the details of Dale's face to express his own obvious joy.

The main image is of Junior celebrating his first few seconds out of the car, arms outstretched in a show of victory. The bottom of the illustration is taken up with the No. 8 Budweiser car blowing by the checkered flag.

I was only half finished with "A Texas Size Win!" when Dale's family came by the studio to see me

a week or so after his funeral. Although I never show work that's in progress (because the finished product will always have more impact), when Dale's mother and sister asked about the painting, I gladly shared it with them. The right half, containing the hug between father and son, was nearly finished, and they were very happy with the emotion it conveyed.

Once Eddie received the finished piece in Texas, he called to tell me how much he liked it. "You still have the belt, Sam," he told me, summing up his feelings in a sports metaphor, meaning I had claimed another victory and retained the heavyweight title. I was tremendously complimented.

The cover was enormously popular with the fans, I think, because it captures a very special moment in time when the competitive torch was shared by two generations. I gave prints as gifts to several of Dale's family members and the team that year.

"...Shadow Of Greatness"
22" x 33", 2002

A while back, TNT aired a commercial with NASCAR drivers talking about drama, which was the network's promotional theme that year. When the camera turned to Dale Jr., there was a quick insert of his father racing and Junior said, "Drama is growing up in the shadow of greatness."

I thought the phrase would make a great title for a painting, even though I didn't have any particular image in mind when I heard it. Such tidbits are usually sources of great inspiration for me. I have used many phrases from music lyrics and song titles in my artwork, so walking around with a headful of unrelated, cool-sounding words is typical for me.

The words "shadow of greatness" gave me the idea to use shading and reflections to reveal the feelings behind Junior's comment on TNT. Budweiser's ad slogan "Run in the Red" inspired me to wash the entire canvas in red, an effect that causes the shadows I used to be more pronounced.

I put the two Earnhardts together in the painting, each in his theme color, which is how Dale became the "shadow" always connected to Junior. The No. 8 Budweiser car casts a reflection, or shadow, of the No. 3 Goodwrench Chevy. Two other very subtle graphic illusions can be found in this piece: the number 8 has a 3 notched out of it, and the car's headlight number also features the 3-inside-the-8 trick.

Because I put so much energy into my work, I can honestly say I'm proud of every painting that bears my name. However, "Shadow Of Greatness…" is one I would have to put on a personal 10 Best list. Considering the emotional weight of Dale's death, I believe it has the strongest impact of any painting I've done.

I'm also proud of it from a technical standpoint. The idea, composition, and execution are all very strong. People tend to stare at this painting for a long time, perhaps realizing there is more to it than first impressions let on. I've seen some fans get very moved as they looked at it. It's a link between past and present for many Earnhardt fans, and the composition bridges that gap forever on canvas.

Occasionally in art, you do something without knowing how you did it. It's like the planets aligned and everything fell into place, making something better than what you thought you were capable of doing. Nothing represents this thought to me more than "Shadow Of Greatness..."

Artists and writers try to get a person to experience what they feel as they are creating a painting or song or novel. When I was painting this, I knew what my idea was and what I was hoping to convey, but then I started working in that zone and, before I realized it, I was looking at the finished piece.

"Red Rocks!"
26" x 22", 2003

Creating an image with one central theme—like a Western piece, for example—is relatively easy and can be very effective at getting across a mood or feeling. Combining multiple themes and wordplay in a single illustration can be trickier.

I started working on a new Dale Jr. painting while at Daytona's Speed Weeks in February 2003; it was actually just a concept drawing at the time. I was aware of Budweiser's love of the color red in its marketing, so I wanted to do a Junior-only piece similar to what I had painted the year before with both Earnhardts in "Shadow Of Greatness…". As I was mulling over different phrases and ideas, the term "red rocks" came to mind.

Since "rocks" can be a noun or a verb, I liked the way the title "Red Rocks!" could be taken as either a description of Mars-like rocks that are red or as an exclamation of action. The rock reference also hints at the rock-star quality Junior has in public and the way his fans treat him.

The background of the painting and most of the other elements are red, although the Martian sky and Earth are depicted in their natural colors. I showed the No. 8 Budweiser car flying like a comet across the surface of the red planet with its fiery tail originating from the middle of the eastern coast of the United States. How many chances would you need to guess that point is Mooresville, N.C.? I'm sure my fellow ZZ Top fans will notice the homage to that group's flying street rods that appeared on album covers and videos.

In his typical too-cool way, Junior is portrayed with shades in place and his baseball cap turned backward. I thought it would be hip and contemporary to present him in that light with that type of a treatment to the composition. This painting brought together several compositional and thematic elements for me. I really enjoy illustrations where there is a play on words in the title.

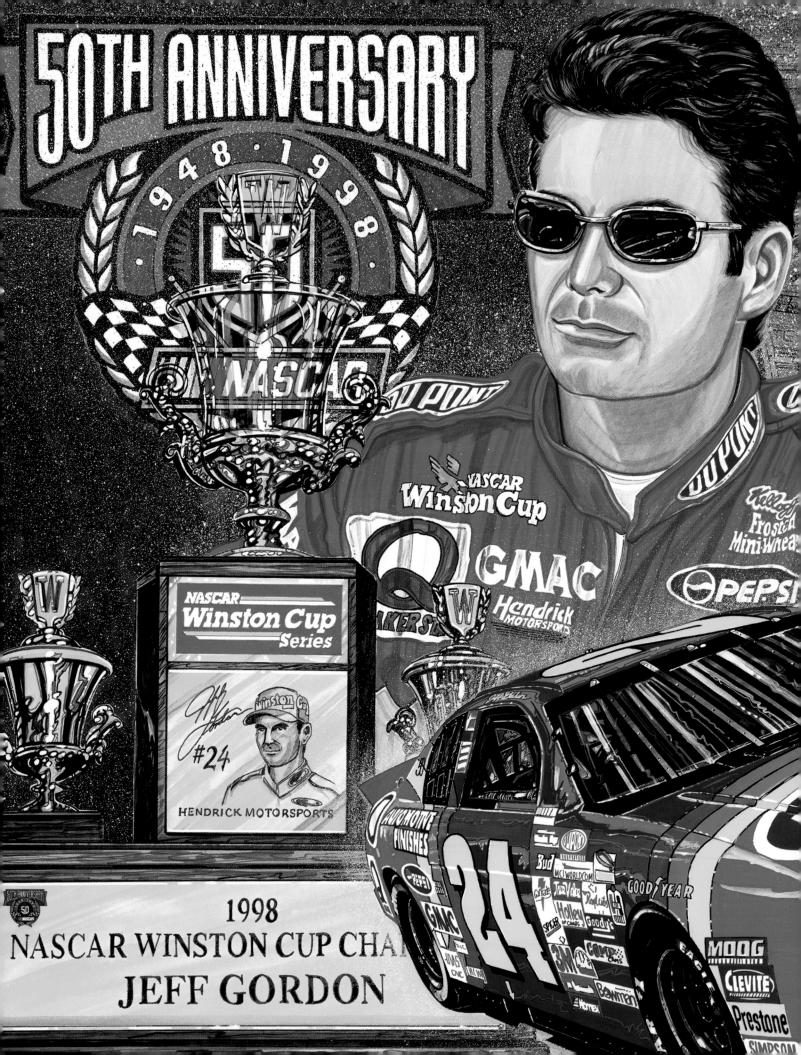

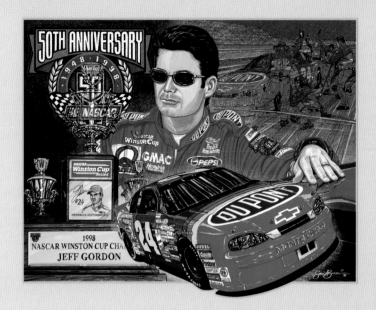

CHAPTER 5:
JEFF GORDON

The story of Jeff Gordon is also the story of NASCAR's explosive growth in the '90s. For me personally, it was the first time in my career that I got to watch a young driver come into the sport and grow into a dominating force.

If anybody ever deserved to reap the benefits of his hard work and dedication, it's Jeff Gordon. Ever since I met Jeff in 1992, just after he moved to North Carolina, I've always thought he was Hollywood's idea of a perfect racer. He's got the looks and he's a well-spoken, talented guy who drives like there's no tomorrow, but it's his ability to always grow into the next phase of his career that has gotten him this far.

A lot of his early success is due, of course, to his stepfather, John Bickford, and his mother, Carol, who adjusted their lives so Jeff could pursue his dream. The Bickfords are great people. I see John often as he works with Action Performance, and I am always proud that Carol visits my gallery when she has guests in town from all over the country.

No one knew what to expect from Jeff when he arrived in the Cup series. Sure, his résumé was packed with driving victories by the time he made it to North Carolina. He was the 1989 USAC Midget Rookie of the Year, then the series champion in 1990. He won the USAC Silver Crown title in 1991, the same year he drove to Rookie of the Year honors in the NASCAR Busch series in a Bill Davis Ford. In 1992, he captured a record 11 pole positions in Busch and signed with Hendrick Motorsports to make the jump to Winston Cup for 1993.

But would he be another hotshot driver who gets swallowed up by the world of Winston Cup?

He was still driving the Baby Ruth car for Bill Davis when we met over lunch. My design work for Jeff was initially orchestrated by Ray Evernham, but Jeff was with us every step of the way as we talked about the designs of his new DuPont car, uniforms, transporters, and other "elements." Jeff had input and voiced his preferences on every aspect of the designs. To this day, whenever I'm in a meeting with him, he's very clear about what he wants to see and doesn't want to see. Since the first DuPont rainbow car, I've done a lot of personal projects for him, including the design of his first Newell coach.

Over the years that followed our first meeting, Jeff won Rookie of the Year honors in Cup, then his first, second, third, and fourth championships. Along the way, he has had a real impact on the public face of NASCAR, probably closing the door forever on the notion that stock car racing is a phenomenon limited to the southeast. He's certainly helped to give it a broader-based commercial appeal.

He's done well with his acting in commercials and appearances on "Saturday Night Live" and talk shows. His talent wins races, but his public persona and clean-cut reputation have won him fans.

In 1999 he established the Jeff Gordon Foundation to support the physical, social, and intellectual needs of children and their families throughout the U.S. His foundation works with four primary established children's charities and various others on a case-by-case basis. I've been happy to contribute work to his foundation, including the Elmo and Cookie Monster fundraising diecast car designs produced in association with the Sesame Workshop.

I'm honored to know and work with Jeff. I meet people in the racing business every day, but very few of them skyrocket into the realm of international celebrity and retain the same sense of humility that he has. It's been really cool to design his Winston Cup cars over the past decade.

"Rookie Sensation!"
17" x 25", 1993

The first painting I did of Jeff and his car was "Rookie Sensation!" How I came to present it to him in person is another one of those funny moments of unusual timing.

Jeff was having so much success in Winston Cup so early in his bid for Rookie of the Year honors that I decided to compose an illustration of him in his helmet, and a portrait with the car in the foreground. The painting would show Jeff wearing the moustache he had sported since his days as a Busch driver. While I was working on it, Ray Evernham phoned to ask if I might do a drawing or something for Jeff's upcoming 22nd birthday party. I told him, "It just so happens I've got this new painting…"

The painting would be done just in time for me to bring Jeff the very first print with an elaborate remarque in the margin. The party was at the old Sandwich Construction Company on Highway 49, a popular hangout for drivers and team members. I was all pumped up.

We were cutting the surprise so close that the ink on the print was still drying as I sat down to create a remarque. I had the frame and matte already cut. Once it was framed, I wrote a note to Jeff on the back, thanking him for being so easy to work with and wishing him a happy birthday.

Off I went to the restaurant, where everybody liked the piece. Jeff walked in, and I immediately saw that he had shaved his moustache!

Ordinarily, that would not concern me much one way or the other, but I had worked like crazy on this painting, and it was outdated the minute I gave it to him—before it even saw the light of day! I wasn't the only one in the group surprised by the change. Evidently, this was very early in his and Brooke's dating relationship, and she asked for the moustache to go.

Later that year, I painted "Top Rookie, '93" to celebrate his upcoming Rookie of the Year win, and that painting was done minus the moustache. The joke around the gallery during that time was to ask people ordering Gordon prints: "Do you want that with or without the moustache?"

Now people hardly remember that he had a moustache when he came onto the circuit. I did a few paintings for sponsor promotions that featured it, but "Rookie Sensation!" is the only one released as a print.

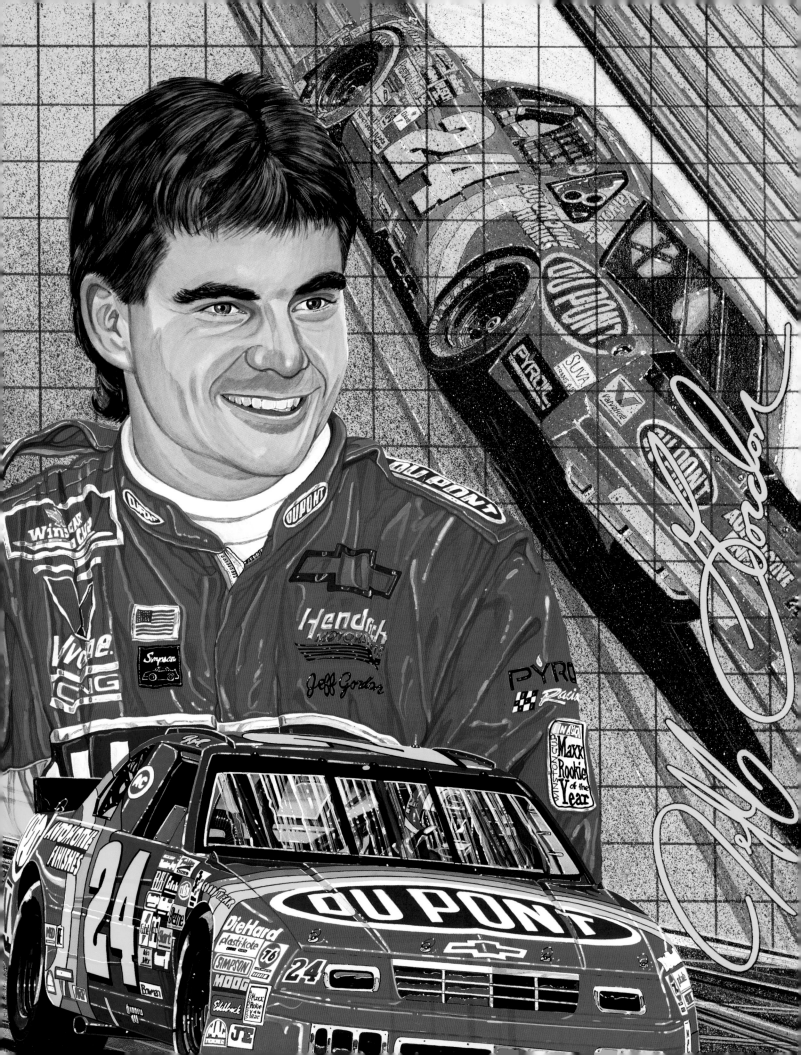

"DuPont Winning Finishes"
30" x 40", 1993

This is probably one of the most comprehensive paintings I've ever done. It shows 21 cars, all of which were painted with DuPont products for the 1993 season. It features a big image of Jeff's car at the top with checkered flags. His corporate teammate, if you will, in the Busch series (running the DuPont car) was Ricky Craven. The painting has a DuPont helmet in the composition, a sky-blue background, the DuPont tag line, and illustrations of other cars—both Busch and Cup—that ran their paints.

This painting took well over 350 hours to execute. DuPont commissioned it, then made a big poster of it. That was pretty special. To have me show their cars through artwork was cool, because they very easily could have done that with photography. They thought it was really special to have the artist who created the paint scheme and had worked so closely with them do their poster.

DuPont doesn't make any watercolor paints I can use for my work, but it would be really awesome if they did.

"Two For One!"

22" x 19", 1995

I was in the press box at Charlotte Motor Speedway in 1994 when Jeff won the Coca-Cola 600, his first NASCAR Winston Cup race. It's a memorable moment to see any new driver score a win, but especially when it happens to such a naturally talented racer as Jeff.

Jeff's driving ability and Ray Evernham's decision to pit for only two right-side tires when the rest of the field was taking longer stops for four put No. 24 in the lead with nine laps to go, a position he never relinquished.

After a brief celebration with his team in victory circle, he was brought up to the press box on suite level, high above the start/finish line, to answer questions from the media.

Even though his interview took place nearly 30 minutes after the race, Jeff was obviously still very emotional and enjoying the moment. I could understand his excitement, since his goal in life had always been to become a world-class racer. That night, at the age of 23, he realized it was going to happen.

Someone in the press asked Jeff what he was thinking during the last lap as he stayed ahead of Rusty Wallace's Ford before taking the checkered flag. Jeff told them frankly that tears were welling up in his eyes as he drove the last lap to win.

When Humpy Wheeler asked me to depict that first victory in a painting for the '95 Unocal banquet, I knew he wanted it to be something special that Jeff and his fans would always remember.

Before I started putting paint to canvas, I had in mind the elements I intended to use. I wanted the background to be dark, like it was during the end of the night race. I wanted to show separate images of Jeff inside his car; the car jacked up on pit road during its last, frenzied stop; and the car crossing the finish line. The Charlotte trophy is recognizable to most race fans because of its unusual design, so I felt it should be incorporated into the illustration. I also wanted to show the number one to indicate it was Jeff's first time to finish first.

I've found that the more elements and "must-haves" I put in a painting, the longer I spend just trying to figure out where everything goes. This piece was no different.

To give a sense of what went on toward the end of the race and what it meant to Jeff, I created a composition where the car crossing the finish line is the foot of the number one. The trophy makes up the vertical part of the number, highlighted against a black background, and you see the final pit stop with the guys working on the car, changing those two critical right-side tires. Up above that, we fade into a scene of Jeff in the car, gripping the steering wheel, and you can see the tear on his face as he takes the final lap. Because of the dominance of the number and the winning tire change, I called it "Two For One!"

The painting itself was huge, and it was the first thing anyone noticed when walking into the foyer of Jeff's corporate office when it was still located at CMS. It was an awesome feeling for me to see my painting in such a prominent place. I especially enjoy visiting a driver's workplace or home and seeing a piece of my art hanging in a place that's personal to them.

CHAPTER 6:
RUSTY WALLACE

If Rusty Wallace and I have one thing in common, it's that Bobby Allison's generosity played a major role in the career successes we've enjoyed. Bobby's driving style and public personality influenced Rusty just as his early support of my work gave me an entrance to the world of NASCAR racing.

It was through our shared mentor that Rusty and I eventually developed a mutually beneficial working relationship.

When Bobby suffered injuries in a wreck at Pocono in June 1988 that put an end to his driving career, the team owner put Dick Trickle in the car for the 1989 season. Trickle won Rookie of the Year honors that season.

Miller Brewing was to move over to Raymond Beadle's team for 1990 and sponsor Rusty's No. 27 Pontiac. When Rusty won the NASCAR Winston Cup championship in 1989, Miller invited Denise and me to New York, which was a huge deal, because it meant we would be attending the awards banquet for the first time. It was great to see Rusty and the rest of the team enjoying their victory.

Back in those days, new team graphics were planned out many months in advance, and you could count on very few changes during the year. I had developed Rusty's 1990 paint scheme during the summer of 1989, which turned out to be one of those giant leaps for my career as a designer. Miller put on a press conference at Charlotte Motor Speedway in November to debut the '90 car and to announce that Rusty would drive for them. The press conference took place in the track's new Speedway Club, with media members and Miller reps watching from suite level as the car was unveiled on pit road. Prints of my painting "Rusty & MGD…1990," which had been commissioned by Miller to celebrate the occasion, were given away.

That event was my first opportunity to meet with Rusty and learn about him and the plans he had for his career. When I finally moved to Concord, Rusty invited me to visit his shop behind the speedway so we could talk and he could show me around. Since then, in addition to my continued working relationship with Miller Brewing, I've also designed a lot of things for Rusty—logos, personal vehicles, and planes. When his brother Kenny started a Busch Series campaign driving for Cox Lumber, Rusty wanted him to have a really professional presentation, so he asked me to create the paint scheme. When he celebrated his 10th anniversary with Miller a few years ago, Rusty asked me to design a special logo he ran on a car in Atlanta to signify the occasion.

Rusty is such an intense person. Whenever I'm working on a project for him, it's not unusual for him to drop by the studio and spend several hours overseeing my work and giving his input. I've learned that Rusty puts that same kind of attention behind everything he does.

Rusty's been a great and supportive friend since that first meeting. As a fan-turned-artist, it was an amazing thing to have a driver who would ask me to stop by his shop to talk about projects. It boosted my confidence and enthusiasm for my chosen career. Because of the respect Rusty has earned on the track, the references and approval he's given my work were no doubt responsible for a lot of the additional work that followed.

You can't put a price on that kind of advertising.

Or on friendship.

"Rusty Wallace, '89 Champion"
21" x 26", 1989

From 1987 to '96, I painted covers for *Winston Cup Illustrated's* commemorative year-end issues. In 1989, as I was watching Rusty secure his hard-fought championship during the final race in Atlanta, the artist part of my brain was thinking, "What am I going to do on the WCI cover?"

Luckily for me, Rusty supplied the inspiration after his victory when he stood up on the roof of his car. After the photographers finished taking pictures of him, he jumped from the roof to the hood to the pavement.

I thought, "That's it, right there!" I immediately sketched Rusty suspended in mid-air between the roof and hood of his car, which was the most dramatic part of his victory celebration. In order to give a clear shot of his winning ride, I showed an overhead of the car with the Kodiak bear on the hood and made the page look like it was ripped, which was pretty dramatic for a publication cover.

"Rusty Wallace, '89 Champion" has always been one of my favorite depictions of Rusty, because it shows such a celebratory action—one of those magic moments in the sport that everybody remembers.

"Rear View Mirror!"

21" x 27", 1990

Ideas for paintings occur to me during the quiet hours when I'm driving to or from a racetrack or heading home for the evening. This probably explains why my artistic output increased dramatically during 1989-1990, when I put 60,000 miles on my car driving from Chester, Va., to Charlotte, N.C.

I was painting and designing full time in Virginia, but all of my business contacts were five hours away in Charlotte. Denise and I were planning to relocate, but it had not happened yet. One of my typical workdays would have me leaving home at 3 a.m., arriving in Charlotte at 8 a.m., and meeting with teams and sponsors all day. If I was lucky, I would pull back into my driveway at home around midnight.

The deadline for the Charlotte Motor Speedway Coca-Cola 600 cover art was approaching, and I had not come across the perfect idea yet. I wanted to incorporate the previous year's on-track skirmish in The Winston, where Rusty Wallace spun Darrell Waltrip and went on to win—giving Darrell his most memorable quote of the year: "I hope he chokes on that $200,000!"

Driving along the Interstate, I was wondering how I could focus on the upcoming Coca-Cola 600 but also conjure the excitement of 1989's Winston. I glanced in my car's rearview mirror, and I had an epiphany. "That's how I'll do it!" I exclaimed to my empty car. Once in front of my drawing board, I put the viewer inside a hypothetical race car following the 1990 cars of Rusty and Darrell. In the rearview mirror, I showed their tangle from 1989 Winston.

There is a framed photo reproduction of that piece in the gallery, although I did not release it as a print. Someone invariably looks at it and comments that it's impossible for a driver to be following and ahead of Rusty and Darrell at the same time.

It's a tough one to explain, I realize, but I thought it was a really cool thing to be looking into your mirror at the past and looking forward at the present.

Although I can't take credit for those rare times I feature a driver on a program cover and he winds up winning the race, I have to admit I wasn't surprised when Rusty won that year's Coca-Cola 600.

One historical footnote has to do with the interior color of the "chase" car in my painting. It was the same green shade as the Mello Yello car that Tom Cruise drove in the movie *Days of Thunder*. During some of my visits to Charlotte in 1990, I stopped by the track to see the filmmaking excitement—some of it must have rubbed off on me.

"Midnight Rider!"
17" x 22", 1992

Usually I have to rack my brain to come up with a concept for a painting, but sometimes the driver I'm depicting does something that makes that part of my job easy.

My assignment was to create a painting for the Richmond program cover in 1992. At the time, one of Rusty's favorite race cars was one he called Midnight Rider. Since Richmond would be a night race and Rusty was the program's featured driver, it made perfect sense to use his car's name and image as the themes in my painting.

Night racing is such an exciting thing to capture on canvas, with the sparks flying and reflections sliding across every hood, roof, and fender. I painted a rear three-quarter view of Midnight Rider in front of the grandstands with a full moon hanging large at the top of the piece. Rusty's image appears in the moon from the perspective of someone peering into the passenger-side window. The result was dark, sleek, and exciting.

Of course, I named it "Midnight Rider!" As the Allman Brothers song of the same name says, "You're not gonna catch him!"

"Monster Slayer!"

21" x 27", 1997

A s with "Midnight Rider," sometimes the easy part of painting is coming up with the idea; the real work comes in figuring out how to make it happen on canvas.

There was a long period of time when I created all the program covers for the four or five events Miller sponsored each year. When the company asked me to dream up something featuring Rusty's No. 2 car taking on Dover Downs in 1997, I saw an opportunity to do something that would really grab the fans' attention.

The track at Dover Downs is nicknamed "Monster Mile," so they have created a T-Rex character called Miles the Monster to match. I thought it would be funny to show Rusty taking on the track in its prehistoric animal form.

In "Monster Slayer!" I depicted Rusty's Ford coming down the track at the title creature exploding out of the asphalt while lightning fiercely streaks across the night sky. The monster is clearly looking for a challenge; its giant jaws are open and ready to swallow up the competition.

I feel like a program cover painting is successful if it gives people something they aren't expecting and it sticks with them after the event, which is why I would consider "Monster Slayer!" a huge success. Obviously, no one has ever taken a picture of a Tyrannosaurus Rex busting up through a racetrack, but when seen in the context of Dover, it works.

I wanted to include that painting in this book because it has so much appeal to children when we take it to shows. When kids come into the gallery, they are fascinated by "Monster Slayer!" They love the monster, and I love that it's not your normal program cover illustration.

"The Eyes Of Texas..."

23" x 27", 1997

When Texas Motor Speedway opened in 1997, I knew it would give me the chance to paint with a lot of southwestern and Wild West imagery. Right away, Miller Brewing Co. asked me to create a print featuring Rusty and commemorating the track's debut season.

The most prominent images are the Texas "Lone Star" flag and Rusty's Miller Lite car approaching the foreground. Inside a silhouette of the state is a closeup of Rusty's face intense with concentration—hence the title, "The Eyes Of Texas..." At the top is my "timeline" of Texas evolution which shows Rusty's car followed by a pistol-waving cowboy and horse at full gallop—both drawn in a style made famous by legendary western artist Frederic Remington.

Because it came at a very busy time of the season, I wound up giving myself a painfully short amount of time to get this painting done. I worked on it for 48 straight hours from beginning to end. Realizing I would be cross-eyed and unable to concentrate at the end of my marathon, I deliberately started with the tight, detailed work, and left the broader strokes for later.

I have to say I surprised myself at how well it was executed.

In addition to the program cover, I created four individual pieces of art for the Fort Worth Star-Telegram that put the drivers' faces and images—Jeff Gordon, Rusty Wallace, Terry Labonte, and Dale Earnhardt—on "Wanted" posters with their cars. The paper printed up these posters with driver bios on the backs and gave them away. That was a really cool promotion. I also created a race preview Sunday supplement for the Star-Telegram.

Of course, the weather didn't care about how much work we and everybody else had put into that inaugural race. It rained enough to set Noah on his way, which killed a lot of the excitement surrounding the event. My brother Rick drove all of our displays and promotional items to Texas from Charlotte—19 hours—just to watch it rain. We didn't get to sell a thing, nor did we do a thing but get wet. However, I'm proud of my role in promoting and commemorating that first Winston Cup race at Texas Motor Speedway.

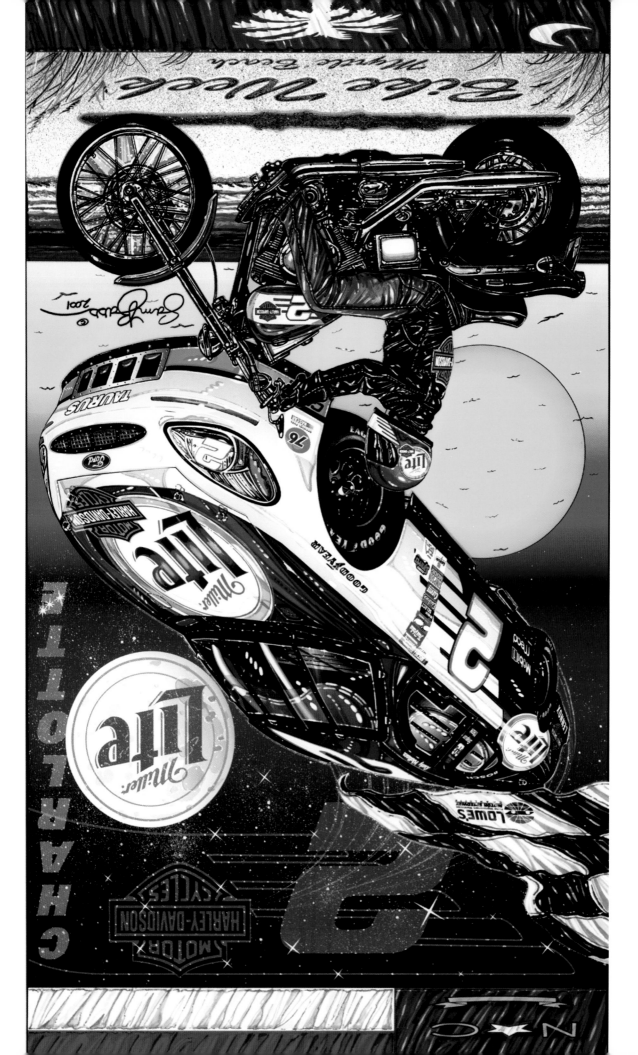

"Two For The Road!"

17" x 29", 2001

When people look through my gallery, they get the impression that I can draw only race cars, drivers, and tracks. I love getting to do projects that are different or unusual for me, such as painting seaweed and ocean plants or the sand—I just don't get a chance to do them that often.

That's why I really enjoyed creating "Two For The Road!" It had several different nonracing elements for me to work with, and there are a few layers of images to discover.

It was commissioned in 2001 by the Mid-Atlantic region of Miller Brewing Co. to link Bike Week in Myrtle Beach, S.C., to The Winston in Charlotte, events that occur over the same week.

The constellation of stars in the sky creates the outline of Rusty's 2, and you can also see the Harley-Davidson logo and wings if you look closely enough. I placed a stylized version of the North Carolina flag at the top of the piece, and I did a similar take on the South Carolina flag at the bottom, represent-ing the host states of these two events.

I split the sky horizontally to show the daytime environment of Bike Week and the nighttime colors of The Winston at Lowe's Motor Speedway—and Rusty's car crosses the line in between the two.

There's a rider on a limited-edition Harley riding along the beach. Considering he's wearing a full-face helmet, it's not hard to tell that I was giving the impression that the rider is Rusty. By the way, Harley-Davidson gave away that bike during a Bike Week promotion.

In the Charlotte logo that runs down the right side of the painting, the E has three starbursts. I cre-ated "Two For The Road!" just a few months after Dale Earnhardt's accident in Daytona. Because he and Rusty were really good friends, I knew Rusty would appreciate it...he did.

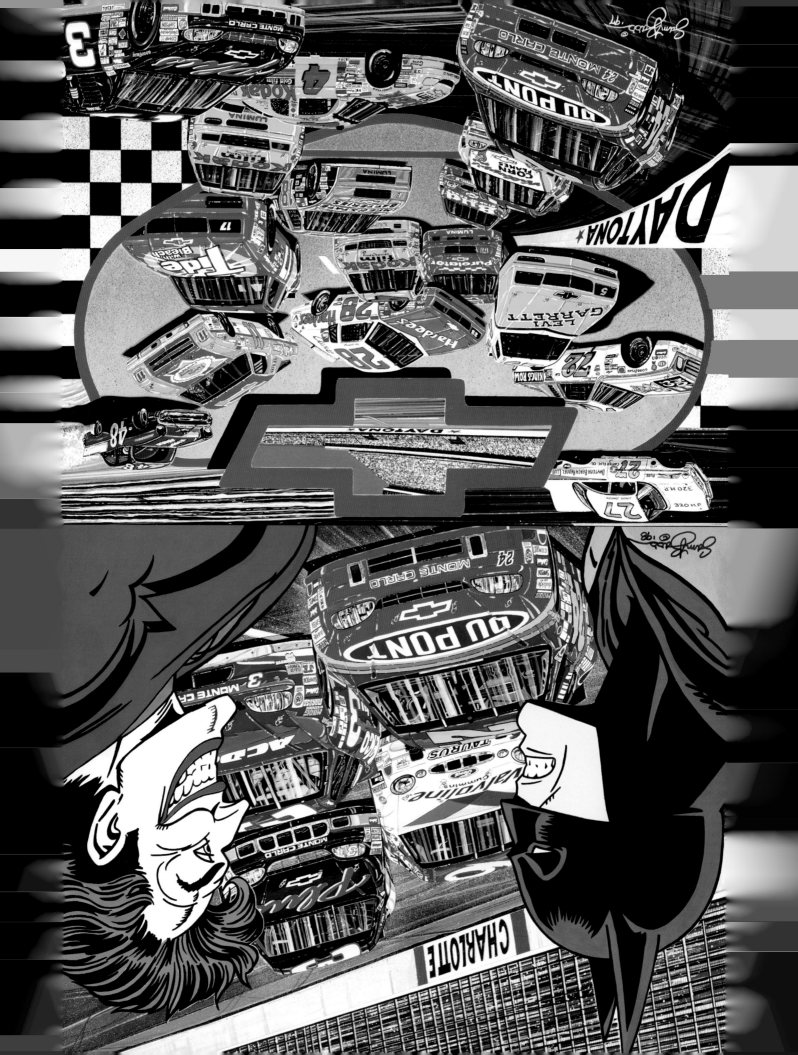

CHAPTER 7:
OTHER DRIVERS &
FAMOUS SUBJECTS

Every day of my life, I have my eyes and ears open for new ideas. I'm always thinking about NAS-CAR, what's going on with the drivers' careers, and what type of paintings I would like to do. Projects often spring from nowhere and get done simply because I would like to take the image from my head and put it on paper.

Other illustration work comes my way from sponsor contacts, public relations representatives, or the drivers themselves making special requests. Usually these jobs result in posters for fans or limited edition prints being given away to VIPs. I would say my workload is divided 50/50 between the self-generated paintings and the special requests.

Commissioned work is all the more special to me when it's for someone's birthday, an anniversary, or a dinner where the recipient and/or subject is being honored. A couple of those special jobs that spring to mind occurred within the past few years.

Steve Harrison and David Hyatt from the Motor Racing Network called to tell me that a dinner honoring Barney Hall's years in broadcasting was scheduled for the weekend of the Fall 2001 Darlington race. They asked if I would be interested in creating a painting showing Barney and some of the race cars that have been significant to him during his illustrious broadcasting career.

One of my many thrills in this business came on a rainy day when I was leaving the infield of Richmond Raceway and saw Barney walking out of the track. He graciously accepted my offer for a ride, and since traffic was slow, I had time to hear a couple of stories from this legend of motorsports radio. One of the great benefits of my job has been that I keep meeting and working with so many of my heroes and people I respect and look up to.

Of course, I immediately said yes to MRN's request.

The main element of my painting was a nice formal portrait of Barney with a headset and microphone, which he uses during every broadcast. Behind him were myriad cars featuring friends he had commented on and watched over the years, all competing against each other. I had been waiting for

Opposite top: "Batman and Joker", 17"x 22", Charlotte, 1998 The Batman and Joker theme of the October 1998 souvenir program cover refers to the entertainment provided during the Lowe's Motor Speedway pre-race show.
Opposite bottom: "Chevy Legends", 17" x 21", 1997. Stock Car Racing magazine commissioned this painting to create a poster that was inserted into the February 1998 issue. A lucky fan won the original in a contest. Right: MRN commissioned this painting to recognize Barney Hall's broadcasting career.

the opportunity to create a very special illustration that would be perfect for my concept of showing the best drivers in NASCAR history—Tim Richmond, Junior Johnson, Bobby Allison, Davey Allison, Cale Yarborough, Dale Earnhardt, and many others competing against one another at their peaks and in their own cars. The theme worked well for Barney's painting, and I intend to expand the idea soon into a painting I call "What If?"

By using a page out of a reporter's notebook, I was able to incorporate into my painting a phrase every race fan identifies with Barney: "This is the finest field of cars we've seen here in a long, long time." It's well documented that he uses that phrase in just about every broadcast. I guess we are to understand that the field gets finer with each passing race.

Barney loved that painting. To this day, whenever I see him he reminds me how much he appreciates the work I did for him. Getting the opportunity to create something that's special and meaningful—not just to the person receiving it, but to the tradition and history of NASCAR—is why I'm such a fan and why I cherish this job.

Another project that took on more meaning than I could know at the time came when the American Cancer Society was honoring Rick Hendrick at a leukemia fundraiser and I was asked by the society to produce a painting for them. They didn't know what to get Rick, because they thought he was sort of hard to buy for. They wanted to know if I would consider painting something.

Rick has been so important to my life and career that I offered to donate my time and services to the charity so they wouldn't have to spend any money on his gift. Since Rick's son Ricky was entering his first year of Busch series competition in the GMAC AC-Delco car, I wanted to create something show-ing the father-son racing tie.

I did a portrait of Rick looking over Ricky's shoulder with the Busch car in the foreground, and Rick helped me unveil it at his dinner. I could tell by his reaction that it was a special image for him.

Later that year Rick commissioned me to make 500 limited edition prints of that painting. Due to a shoulder injury he suffered in a crash, Ricky decided to retire from driving and become a car owner on the Busch circuit. I'm sure he'll grow into a leadership role at Hendrick Motorsports some day, because he's very involved in the operation his father put together and turned into a racing empire. When Ricky becomes known as a car owner in years to come, he'll be able to look at my painting and remember the brief period right before he decided to follow in his father's footsteps.

"Richard Petty Blueprint"

24" x 24", 1988

It's ironic that the first limited edition print I ever produced from one of my paintings was not of my boyhood idol Bobby Allison, but of his archrival Richard Petty. Until that time my art income had been strictly from commissions and selling original paintings, but I was eager to feel out the market for high-quality reproductions.

In 1988 I painted "Richard Petty Blueprint," playing up the fact that Richard was the only driver I've ever heard of who had a color named for him, Petty Blue. The painting is a juxtaposition of Richard's car in the foreground on a steep bank and something like a designer's blueprint highlighting the nose of a new Pontiac Grand Prix coming at the viewer. My blueprint theme was also a nod to the newness of that Grand Prix design—it wasn't actually on the road yet when I started the project—and I knew Pontiac would appreciate a beauty shot of its new car.

The reference photo I used for the painting was of the same Grand Prix that Richard ran in Daytona in '88, where he rolled violently several times down the track's front stretch.

I have to say I was happy with the results of that painting, and I decided it would be the first to be sold as a print. I sent images of the piece to Petty Enterprises for Richard's approval and authorization. Denise and I unveiled "Richard Petty Blueprint" at Richard's annual Fourth of July open house, a giant fan club event, so we were with the right people to gauge interest. It was one of the hottest days I've ever experienced in North Carolina, but we kept rolling posters for those Petty fans.

For the first time in my career, I had a product to market other than original paintings. The response we got from that first effort really put my little business on the map.

Right: A detail from "Things Kings Are Made Of," shown on page 111.

"Believe me when I say it's easier to paint a perfect car than it is to show a badly damaged one that has parts flying off in every direction."—Sam Bass

"Things Kings Are Made Of"
26" x 22", 1992

Summing up "King" Richard Petty's career in one painting would be enough to intimidate any artist, but when Gwaltney Foods asked me to create a historical painting in 1992 for Petty's Fan Appreciation Tour, I jumped at the chance. It was a challenge to figure out what elements would go where and how the eye would move from one thing to another.

Since the painting would be composed of Petty's racing memories, I thought the title "Things Kings Are Made Of" was appropriate. The background of the piece—the thematic glue that held everything else together—was a side shot of his '92 Pontiac from the driver's side door. Below that are the tops of his seven Winston Cup trophies.

I took some artistic license with my depiction of the trophies, which in real life, looked different each year but were identical in the painting. My reason for this change was to avoid the impression that the viewer was looking at a collection of trophies from different races. I also thought the seven awards all together made a stronger visual statement.

Next to the No. 43 I placed Petty's Charlie One Horse cowboy hat and sunglasses, two accessories he's rarely seen without in public. Over those images I worked in items that were key to his career, such as a newspaper clipping of the 1976 Daytona 500 finish between him and David Pearson. Even though Petty lost that race to Pearson, the dramatic finish went down in history as one of the most thrilling in Winston Cup history. It may seem unusual to put a memory of a "non-victory" into a driver's painting, but Petty fans fondly remember that event as a highlight in The King's career.

Petty's first Winston Cup car is on hand, as is his final '92 model. Complementing the first and last cars are reproductions of tickets to those races. There's a nostalgic black and white shot of the Plymouth in which he won 27 races and 19 poles during the 1967 season, as well as his famous Charger.

Although I just about never depict wrecks in my paintings, my favorite part of "Things Kings Are Made Of" would have to be the spinning, tumbling turns I re-created of his legendary 1988 Daytona 500 crash. That image of the car turning airborne pirouettes down the front stretch fence is essential for any visual history of Richard's career. It was used in magazine and television ads, and even shown repeatedly by David Letterman when Petty appeared on his show. Believe me when I say it's easier to paint a perfect car than it is to show a badly damaged one that has parts flying off in every direction. Capturing the sense of motion gone out of control was my goal.

"Underbird"

21" x 27", 1992

Underbird" is another painting that includes hidden elements, just waiting to be discovered.

I created the piece to celebrate Alan Kulwicki's 1992 championship season, and I decided to build it around the driver's self-proclaimed underdog status. Alan was proud of how he had accomplished so much with much fewer resources than most of his competition on The Winston Cup circuit.

His personal icon was the Mighty Mouse cartoon character, and he wore a patch of the character on his uniform, which I designed for him. I knew I had to feature the mouse prominently in my painting, but I also put a subtle rendering of the character in the reflection of Alan's championship trophy. It's pretty clear to people once they notice it in the bell of the trophy, but I'm surprised how much time it takes some folks to see it.

Alan also had a clever way of turning his race car into a personal statement by leaving the letters "Th" out of his Thunderbird's bumper lettering so that it read "Underbird." I made sure the car in the painting repeated his little inside joke.

I'm always happy to put something in a painting that can bring people back again and again. Sadly, I did not have a chance to spend very much time with Alan before his death less than a year later, but I know that in his short time on the circuit, his determination and talent as a driver earned him some extremely loyal fans.

"Harry Gant '93"

21" x 24", 1993

Harry Gant is one of those people you want to be when you grow up. Down-to-earth, sincere, and talented, he's just one of the coolest drivers I've ever dealt with, and he's an inspiration to anybody who desires to age gracefully. Harry was doing things on the track against drivers 15 years his junior and putting a hurt on them week in and week out, yet I was surprised to find that he remained so humble about it.

I did a lot of work for U.S. Tobacco in the early '90s, on their press kits, car designs, and promotional illustrations. Actually, I created "Harry Gant '93" to be used as a press kit cover, and I released it as a limited edition print later on.

One of my all-time career highlights was signing autographs with Harry at a car dealership in North Carolina. I had seen him during races and at press functions, but I never had a free moment to talk to him. During our autograph session, we spent a couple of hours talking, and I was so impressed by what a genuine person he was.

I was just the guy drawing pictures, but he treated me like I was family or, better yet, like another driver. He talked to me the whole time we were signing posters, prints, hats, and everything else fans came up with. I had been in Charlotte for only three years at that time, and to be accepted by somebody of his stature in that manner was really awesome.

When you are on the receiving end of someone else's generosity and good manners, it really reminds you to watch how you treat other people. I think all drivers should use Harry's public behavior as a standard to work toward.

"4-Ever Champions"

26" x 26", 1993

The end of the 1993 Winston Cup season in Atlanta was a powerfully bittersweet moment. Dale Earnhardt and Rusty Wallace had fought the fiercest battles of their careers leading up to that final lap, with Dale winning his seventh championship and Rusty taking home the trophy for the race.

Ordinarily the fans would be out of their minds with excitement over the close outcome of the season, but weighing heavily on their hearts were the losses of Davey Allison and Alan Kulwicki, both of whom had been killed in aviation accidents during the year.

Emotions were high for the traditional victory laps of race and season champions, but when Dale unfurled a No. 7 flag (representing Alan's car number as well as Dale's seventh championship) and Rusty brought out a No. 28 flag (Davey's number), there wasn't a dry eye in the grandstands. The two winners turned their cars around and did Alan Kulwicki's "Polish victory lap" in tribute to the late drivers.

As I was watching this, very much caught up in the moment, I was thinking, "This is so powerful! I've got to convey this moment of loss and celebration in a painting!" I wasn't going to do anything without talking to Dale and Rusty first to gauge their reactions. I didn't want people in the industry to think I was trying to benefit from an emotional moment. When we talked, I told them I would donate the proceeds to Speedway Children's Charities, and that I felt it was an appropriate way to honor the memories of Alan and Davey.

I sketched a quick drawing of my idea, showing Dale and Rusty doing their reverse victory lap and the two fallen competitors racing wheel to wheel in the sky. I faxed it to dale and Rusty and they signed off on it that week.

I was able to give the crews of the four respective cars limited edition prints of the painting and make a sizeable donation to SCC, but I think the real sense of accomplishment came from giving the fans of these drivers a reminder of what they meant to us while they were here.

"Thunderbat!"

21" x 28", 1995

I was a tremendous fan of Batman when I was growing up. I read the comic book, watched the television show and cartoons, and saw the movie several times.

When McDonald's and the producers of *Batman Forever* put together a cross-promotional agreement to feature the Dark Knight himself on Bill Elliott's car (turning his Thunderbird into a "Thunderbat"), I knew I had to do a painting of it.

Once my licensing was cleared, I was offered approved images of Batman to incorporate into my painting. I chose to show Bill Elliott in his full helmet with no visible facial features because I wanted his appearance to be dark and mysterious—as Batman-like as possible.

I included a cool running shot of the Thunderbat on the track with a reflection in the pavement of the Batmobile. Over the night sky was the image of the bat signal, suggesting there was a dire emergency involved.

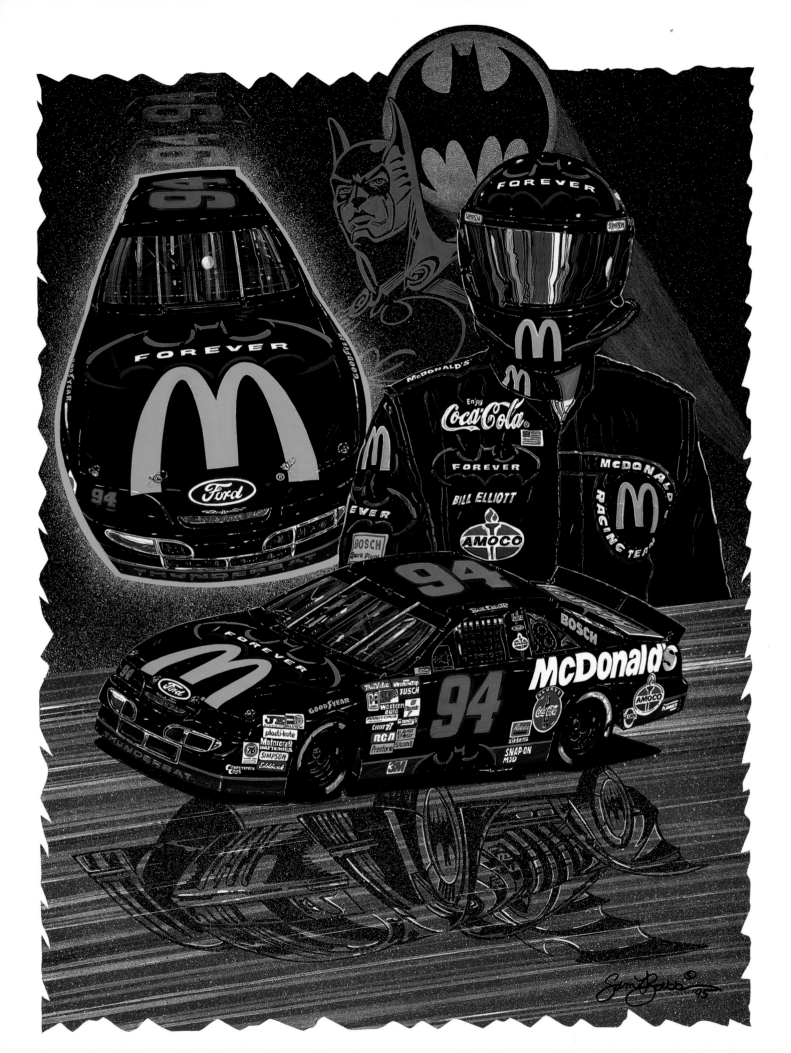

"Silver & Gold"

21" x 26", 1996

At the end of 1996 I wanted to capture two memorable events from Terry Labonte's career in one painting: his record for most consecutive Winston Cup starts and his win of the series championship.

Terry's No. 5 Chevrolet Monte Carlo was wearing a special silver paint scheme when he made his 513th consecutive start in the First Union 400 at North Wilkesboro that year (which he won from the pole), matching Richard Petty's then-record streak. The following week, also driving the silver car, he established a new record by starting the Goody's 500 at Martinsville.

Terry, who had claimed his first Winston Cup championship 12 years earlier, won only two races in '96 (the other being the fall Charlotte 500-miler), but that was enough to clinch the title.

It was clear to me that the silver car and gold championship trophy would inspire my title and should be featured prominently. I depicted Terry as he appeared at the end of the NAPA 500 in Atlanta, giving the "number one" sign. (In one of those great NASCAR moments, Terry's brother Bobby won the Atlanta race, so both Labontes took a victory lap.)

To commemorate the record, I had 514 limited edition prints made. When Kellogg's featured my painting of its champion driver on a cereal package, the company sent me a small stack of flat boxes, which I autographed and sent to the first 12 customers who bought a print of "Silver & Gold."

"Touchdown!"

21" x 31", 1996

've been a Washington Redskins fan since I was 7 years old. When former Redskins coach Joe Gibbs brought his considerable talents to Winston Cup racing, I anticipated great things from him. He won right away with Dale Jarrett and later hired driver Bobby Labonte.

Bobby's first Cup win was at Charlotte Motor Speedway's Coca-Cola 600 in 1995, when he and older brother Terry pulled off a picture-perfect one-two finish. The next year, when I was asked to create a painting for the Unocal dinner honoring Bobby as the returning race champion, I already had my theme figured out.

I could not resist the urge to compare racing to football, given the Gibbs connection; it was such a natural tie-in. In football the goal is a touchdown; in racing, it's to cross the finish line first. Victory circle became the end zone, and Bobby was a player celebrating a game-winning touchdown.

I had to take some artistic liberties with Bobby's image to make the football comparison work. The photos I had of him in victory lane showed him hoisting the trophy with one hand while his other arm was naturally by his side. In order to make the football metaphor complete, I had him raising his other arm as well, which poses him in the universal touchdown celebration stance as if he's saying: "Through the uprights! We're number one!"

Behind and to the side of Bobby is a portrait of Gibbs looking on proudly, the trophy looming large, and a shot of the No. 18 Interstate Batteries car in victory circle with Bobby's Carolina Panthers helmet sitting on the hood. In the foreground is a shot of Bobby on his last lap with Terry hot on his bumper.

The team loved it, and I was authorized to make a limited edition reproduction of the painting, with Joe and Bobby both signing the prints. To show my enthusiasm for their win, I gave a portion of the prints to the team. As a Redskins fan, getting to do something for Joe Gibbs was very meaningful and its own reward. Bobby is also one of the nicest people I've met in NASCAR and a great person to be around. I think he's a real asset to the sport.

"We're Ready!"
20" x 26", 2002

One of the things I enjoy most about my career is the chance to work with young, up-and-coming drivers. At 41 years of age, I don't feel in any way that I'm an old guy, but along the way I've had the chance to meet a lot of the younger racers and do design work for them.

In 2001 Lowe's Home Improvement Warehouse asked me to submit designs for a new corporate look that would debut on a car Hendrick was building for its newest driver, Jimmie Johnson. Between me and the other illustrators who were considered, Lowe's reviewed more than 45 different designs before finally accepting mine. I designed Jimmie's car, transporter, uniform, helmet, and team uniforms.

I attended the press announcement at Lowe's Motor Speedway, where Jimmie and teammate/car owner Jeff Gordon unveiled the new car. When the 2002 season started, Jimmie immediately proved his value to the Hendrick stable by winning his 13th Winston Cup race, the NAPA Auto Parts 500 at California Speedway. At the end of the season, Jimmie had a total of three wins to his credit and finished fifth in points overall. His car was voted one of the top 10 new paint schemes for 2002.

I immediately painted "We're Ready!" shortly after Jimmie's first win, borrowing the title from a line he delivered in a Lowe's television commercial. The folks at Lowe's printed 130,000 posters of the image, and gave one to each employee.

The painting, which is decorated liberally with flying confetti, showed Jimmie doing a burnout after the race, a portrait of the driver with his arms raised in victory circle, and a beauty shot of his car crossing the finish line.

It's great to meet drivers without knowing much about them at first, and then to see them achieve great success on the track. I enjoy the small role I play in that, and hope I've contributed something special by giving them a nice-looking race car that their fans are excited about.

"Million Dollar Smile!"
25" x 27", 2002

Mark Martin commissioned "Million Dollar Smile!" after his hard-fought win during the 2002 Coca-Cola Racing Family 600 at Lowe's Motor Speedway. The victory brought with it a $1 million bonus as part of the No Bull 5 competition. In his postrace interviews, Martin repeatedly credited the hard work performed by his shop and pit crews with making the win possible.

Afterward, his agent, Benny Ertel, called to tell me that Mark wanted a special painting commemorating the win to give his crew guys. That win had ended a losing streak and gave the team momentum for a title chase. It was a tremendous honor to be asked, but it was all the more special to me that Mark was so appreciative of his crew.

I worked on "Million Dollar Smile!" through the rest of 2002 and had 50 limited edition prints produced on chrome paper. Mark had them framed and gave them as Christmas presents to the crew. I know it was well received because I have gotten many comments and compliments from individual team members.

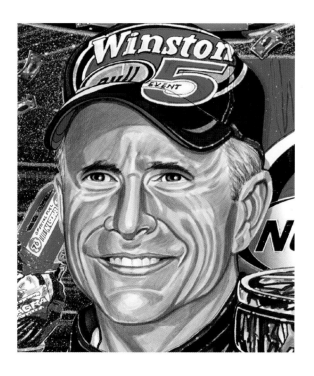

"The Burning Of Atlanta!"

22" x 17", 2003

To my surprise, Atlanta Motor Speedway asked me to feature Tony Stewart on the cover of its 2003 Bass Pro Shops MBNA 500 cover as the defending race winner from the 2002 event and the 2002 Winston Cup champion.

I was surprised because Tony's sponsor, Home Depot, is the main competitor for Lowe's Home Improvement Warehouse, which has a strong official status at the Speedway Motorsports, Inc. tracks. I didn't even artistically hide the Home Depot logo, as is a common request when one sponsor wins on another sponsor's home turf.

My layout for the painting centers around Tony doing a spectacular victory burnout on the finish line, with two funnel-shaped clouds of smoke rising out of the celebration. In one section is a portrait of Tony in his sunglasses and uniform; the other smoke column was the background for an image of the trophy he had just won. The smoke clouds were significant, maybe even symbolic, because Tony's nickname is Smoke.

Because I wanted my title to suggest that Tony's hard-fought win and championship were the result of a powerful, unstoppable force, I reached into Civil War history and came up with "The Burning Of Atlanta!" (Associating racing moments with overwhelming military force is not uncommon. You may recall the "E-Day" campaign that accompanied Dale Earnhardt Jr.'s entry into Winston Cup.)

I have to admit I borrowed from myself with the smoky cloud theme. I had used a similar concept just a few months earlier, when I painted the championship illustration for Larry Dixon and his dragster. I really liked the way it worked, so I put it to use with Tony.

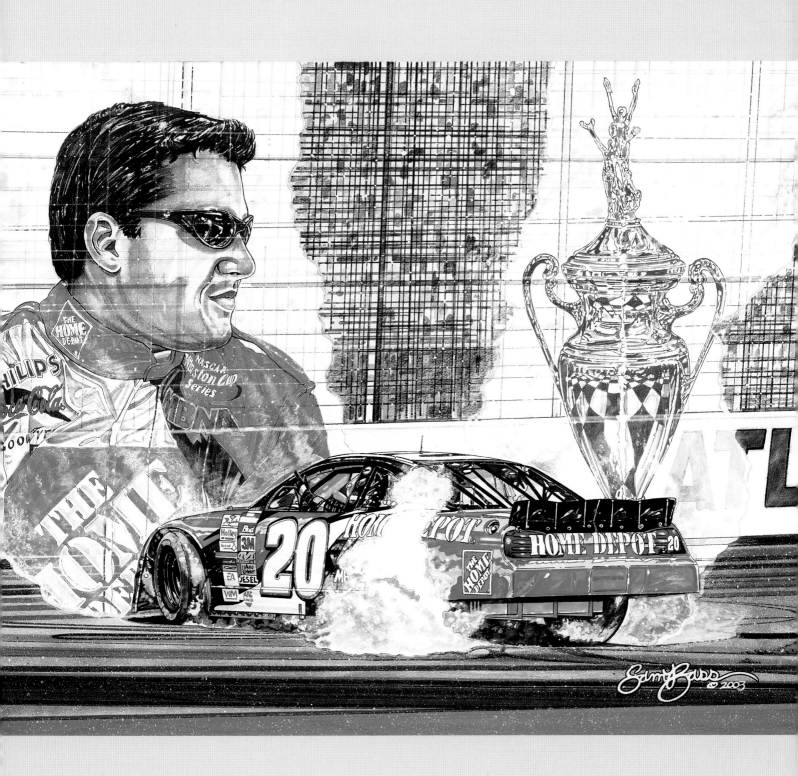

"D.W. Farewell Tour"

13" x 17", 2000

As much as Darrell Waltrip had given to the sport of stock car racing during his three decades as a driver, it was with some regret that I worked on projects marking his retirement in his 2000 farewell season. D.W.'s resume is a long list of records and accomplishments that deserved recognition, including 84 Winston Cup victories, 59 Winston Cup poles, and five Coca-Cola 600 wins, to name a few.

D.W. has always been a fan favorite, and as a big fan myself I was honored to design the paint scheme for the final Cup car he would drive in competition, which incorporated a flame concept.

Atlanta Motor Speedway asked me to create a program cover devoted entirely to Darrell for its season-end race. I kept it simple—a nice portrait of the driver and several of the cars that had been significant to his stellar career.

Darrell really liked that piece, because he had me design a variation of it for use on an autograph card that he's been using ever since. It was a special request from Darrell that meant a lot to me, knowing his fans would have him sign thousands of them—all with one of my illustrations featured on the front.

"Western Auto/AC-Delco Racing, '91"

17" x 22", 1991

Western Auto commissioned this painting for a national marketing promotion that featured Darrell Waltrip.

CHAPTER 8:
PROGRAM COVERS

I don't know when the race program became the colorful, slick magazine that it is today, but the origins of that useful event souvenir go back further into history than most of us realize.

I read an article by a historian who had devoted a great deal of time to researching the early years of the Coliseum in Rome. Once a wonder of the ancient world, the Coliseum was not too different from the modern superspeedway. In fact, a race fan from today might have felt right at home in its seats. Spectators attending gladiatorial battles, chariot races, and other spectacles enjoyed the amenities of indoor plumbing, luxury suites, concession stands, roving food vendors, and even an early scorecard outlining the day's planned events and a listing of major participants.

About 2,000 years later, circa late 1960s, souvenir programs had improved somewhat, but most were printed in black and white on very cheap paper and were packed with as many ads from local businesses as the promoter could sell. The program I bought during my first visit to Richmond's Southside Speedway was a very simple affair packed with information about competitors and the requisite local ads, but what caught my attention most was the one part the publisher had obviously spent a few dollars to improve: the cover. It featured a colorful illustration of several race cars—an image that, at my impressionable age, I thought was high art. I had already spent a lot of time drawing things for fun, but it had not occurred to me yet that something I created could someday be used on the front of a race program.

Fast-forward again to 1984 to find me in Concord, N.C., sitting outside the office of Charlotte Motor Speedway President H.A. "Humpy" Wheeler with a portfolio of my work. I had driven down from Virginia to pitch the track on hiring me to illustrate its program covers. My visit was unplanned and not on anyone's meeting schedule; my youthful enthusiasm didn't understand appointments. I found the speedway offices (which, would become my offices a few years later upon completion of the 7-story Smith Tower) and walked in to see if I could talk to someone in charge of souvenir programs.

In what turned out to be the luckiest bit of timing in my life, Coca-Cola had just signed on to sponsor the spring 600-mile race, and Humpy was open to ideas that would raise people's quality perceptions of the facility and its events. In other words, like any good promoter, he wanted to make them feel as though they had gotten their money's worth, and that impression began with their first purchase on entering the speedway: a program.

I was hired to provide the '85 Coca-Cola 600 program cover and, 40 program cover paintings later,

I'm still the artist of record.

In working on my first painting for CMS, I dealt with several people who had input on every little detail of sponsor placement and other concerns. After that first job I earned their confidence, and a really comfortable situation developed whereby they trusted me to work within their parameters and turn out a painting that would make everybody happy. Some of the work I'm most proud of is art that's been done for Charlotte covers, because of the creative freedom they allowed me.

I don't believe any other artist has been fortunate enough to develop such a solid working relationship with a speedway, and I will always owe track owner Bruton Smith, Humpy Wheeler, and public relations department heads Tom Cotter, Eddie Gossage, and Jerry Gappens a debt of gratitude for giving me the chance to prove myself.

"Into The New"
17" x 22", Richmond, 1988

Because Richmond was my home track for years before I relocated to Charlotte, it was only a matter of time before I convinced track owner Paul Sawyer to use one of my paintings as a program cover.

I met Mr. Sawyer in 1982 when I also dropped by his office unannounced to talk about creating artwork for his track. This was not too long after my weekend in Talladega from which I took home three new commissions, so my confidence and ambition were building. He not only met with me, but he agreed to provide a garage credential for the Richmond race so I would not have to talk my way through security like I had in Alabama.

When I first talked to Mr. Sawyer, I was still just a college student who hoped to go into the art business someday, but with his characteristic graciousness he treated our talk as though I occupied a much higher place on the corporate food chain. I was eager to repay his kindness, so I was pleased when he asked me to create a new logo for the fairground track.

A few years later, NASCAR had outgrown a lot of the small tracks that once were its bread and butter, and Paul had no intention of Richmond losing its stock car races. In late February 1988 the old half-mile fairground speedway held its last race to make way for a new three-quarter-mile Richmond International Raceway.

Paul also asked me to commemorate the occasion with a painting for the track's first program cover. Called "Into The New," it featured an eye-catching transition from the old fairgrounds in black and white to the new speedway in color. Bobby Allison's 1988 Miller Buick, which I designed, and teammate Bobby Hillin's car are driving from the old track to the new, going from a rickety guardrail to a nice, new solid wall sporting the new logo I created for Mr. Sawyer.

"Into The New" was significant to me in another way, because it marked the second time one of my paintings was produced as a limited edition print. Miller ordered 400 of them to be given away to VIPs during the special September weekend when the new facility opened.

"Legendary Reflections"

17" x 22", Charlotte, 1991

t's a real pleasure to get feedback about a painting from fans. Because 30,000 or more people might buy souvenir programs, a compelling image of mine on the cover tends to get a lot of response.

Such was the case with "Legendary Reflections," which I created for Charlotte Motor Speedway's May 1991 races. The painting looks simple enough at first. Earnhardt, Petty, and Wallace are tearing up the track and showing no mercy to their competitors. Upon a second glance at the pavement below, the actions of this talented trio are matched tire for tire by the reflections of three '60s-era drivers and cars.

Humpy had arranged to have a pre-race show for The Winston called "Winston Legends" featuring some of the greatest retired drivers who ever raced at Charlotte. The idea behind my painting was to show the modern racers in fierce competition while reminding everyone in a subtle way that drivers are the same in every generation.

Reactions to that painting were very strong. People called me months after it ran to let me know they had just noticed the cars in the reflections. It was often the case that the vintage cars were not seen until accidentally viewed with the program turned upside down.

Sometimes it can be tedious to do work that is so subtle in its meaning, but I enjoy creating images that reveal deeper layers as you study them.

"Into The Night!"
19" x 24", Charlotte, 1992

Working with Charlotte Motor Speedway (now Lowe's Motor Speedway) is never boring! There is always something wild going on in there that Humpy wants to promote or celebrate on the program cover, and I'm happy to oblige.

Humpy's dream of illuminating the 1.5-mile superspeedway for nighttime racing was finally realized in 1992, and I chose to depict the excitement of the first-ever artificially lighted running of The Winston with my painting "Into The Night!"

The best way to show off something new is to contrast it directly with something old, so I split the canvas into light and dark halves. I placed Dale Earnhardt, the first driver on the track for nighttime practice sessions, at the lead of a pack of cars heading into the speedway's Turn One. Half of the cars were set in natural light, and half were depicted under the artificial night lighting. Centered at the top of the canvas is a giant orb that is half sun and half moon.

Technically, it was a difficult image to create due to the distorted perspective and lighting issues and the challenge of getting everything to work around the split canvas idea, but when it was done Humpy said it was one of the nicest sports illustrations he had ever seen, because it really defined the moment.

"Royal Memories!"

26" x 23", Charlotte, 1992

From a graphics standpoint, I think the globe-and-car icon that represents Lowe's Motor Speedway and parent company, Speedway Motorsports Inc., is really strong. Circles and ovals are already good design elements for logos because they suggest an entire world is served or dominated in some way by a company; putting that generic speeding car in the middle of it symbolically tells everyone, "We are the center of the racing world!"

For the October 1992 race at Charlotte, I was asked to paint something that would recall and pay tribute to the unmatched career of retiring seven-time Winston Cup champion Richard Petty—all with a home-track slant.

I started with the famous globe and broke it down into its individual components, then filled each with paintings of historical Petty images and cars. It was quite a challenge, as I had to paint each section the way it's divided and allow for the negative space in between, but still make the illustration carry from one defined geometric shape to the other without losing continuity.

I titled the piece "Royal Memories!" and was honored to get to unveil and present it to Richard at a press conference at the speedway.

"Sundown Showdown!"

29" x 25", Charlotte, 1993

Second to racing, Humpy Wheeler's passion in life is boxing. Humpy is a former amateur boxer, and he has devoted part of the speedway's second floor to the Carolinas Boxing Hall of Fame. That said, I knew my idea to pattern 1993's "Sundown Showdown!" after a promotional boxing poster would be a one-two knockout punch.

Because Charlotte has had two May races—The Winston and the Coca-Cola 600—each year since I started painting covers (other than the year The Winston was held in Atlanta), I've always had the challenge of making one illustration promote, commemorate, or look back on two different events.

I started running through layout ideas in my head and on paper, looking for a fresh way to convey the excitement of the two different races. The focus of the painting would be an incident that took place a split second after the end of the previous year's Winston.

Kyle Petty, driving the Mello Yello car, and Davey Allison, driving for Texaco Havoline, were fighting so hard for the finish line that Davey spun and crashed backward into the retaining wall just as he won the race. His celebration had to wait until his return from the hospital. Ordinarily, I will not paint a crash scene because I feel very strongly that the safety of the drivers should be every fan's concern, and I don't want to contribute any idea to the contrary. Because Davey did not suffer severe or permanent injuries, I felt that to ignore this scene would make the topic conspicuous by its absence and rob the fans of the previous event's excitement.

People always expect a showdown any time two drivers tangle on the track, so I placed Kyle and Davey center stage in the painting, with their reflective helmet visors replaying the '92 finish. This is a look I borrowed from the typical boxing match poster, wherein the combatants are shown in strong profile trying to stare each other down. In boxing posters, you can only guess what's on the minds of the two men; with "Sundown Showdown!" it's obvious Kyle remembers the competition taking place right before the wreck, and Davey has a slightly different take on the race. In the background is a look across Charlotte's front stretch during the Coca-Cola 600, where you can clearly see the sun setting behind a row of luxury suites.

After this piece appeared on the program cover and as a limited edition print from my gallery, I noticed a new emphasis on helmet designs in the NASCAR T-shirt and racing collectibles industry. Open-wheel racing had always played up wildly painted helmets as part of the too-cool aspect of its drivers.

I've sometimes wondered if it was just a coincidence or if my decision to prominently feature two very colorful helmet paint schemes had any influence on that trend. When a driver puts on a well-designed full-face helmet and reflective shield, I think it gives him a tough, spaceman kind of look. There's an intriguing atmosphere that surrounds you when people can't read your facial expressions or eyes. I think I captured that mystique in "Sundown Showdown!"

"The Heat Is On!"

25" x 18", Charlotte, 1996

Is there any image in racing more thrilling than four cars running side by side at full speed on a track just wide enough to accommodate them? The great thing about being an artist is that I can create such moments, even if they never happened.

"The Heat Is On!" is a powerful example of the four-wide horizontal format, where the cars of Dale Earnhardt, Jeff Gordon, Terry Labonte, and Dale Jarrett fill the frame from left to right. The speedway's P.R. department head, Jerry Gappens, and I decided the painting should feature the four top drivers in points going into the UAW-GM Quality 500 at Charlotte that year.

To me, the image of the four facing the viewer with arms crossed atop the separate illustration of the cars says, "We're battling each other, and we're bringing this show to you!" I put a heated glow around the cars in order to indicate how intense the battle for the championship was that year.

Everything about this image speaks directly to the viewer, so it's impossible for a race fan to see it without being engaged in the action.

The folks at Kellogg's were so intrigued with the painting—and the prominent placement of their driver, Terry—that they asked to use it on a three-package series of collectible cereal boxes. The image was split up so Earnhardt appeared on a box by himself; Jeff and Terry were on a box together; and Jarrett had the third box. Fans were encouraged to buy all three because they could be put together to create the whole image.

I remember being overjoyed when I walked into my local grocery store and saw the end-of-aisle displays featuring my artwork.

"Fireworks!"

17" x 22", Charlotte, 1997

Anniversaries make people stop and think for a second about how far they've come and how successful they've been in achieving their goals. When Darrell Waltrip's 25th year as a driver came around in 1997, the public relations department at Charlotte asked me to commemorate the occasion in my program cover painting.

Rather than do a simple head-and-car shot of D.W., I wanted to incorporate more of the race-week action into the painting. I composed everything so the viewer is looking at Turn 2 into the new Diamond Tower Terrace grandstands. The point of view is of a driver in a pack of cars being led by Dale Earnhardt, with a clear look at the stands where D.W.'s No. 17 Western Auto Chevrolet is seen as a projection of the speedway's massive spotlight into the middle of a fireworks display.

There was a special prerace show in D.W.'s honor, and I gave him the painting in front of the whole speedway crowd. That presentation was a special event in my career. I don't think I ever had that many people watching me do something live before.

Above: An original illustration of the chrome paint scheme of Darrell Waltrip's car that celebrated Waltrip's 25 years in NASCAR racing.

"LMS 2000"

17" x 22", Charlotte, 2000

LMS 2000" is a good example of what happens when design decisions haven't been finalized as we go to press with a program cover featuring a certain car.

In The Winston, Dale Earnhardt was running his wild Peter Max design, and Jeff Gordon was celebrating a new contract with DuPont by driving a car we referred to as "Signature" because it was signed by the driver, team owner, and sponsor. I designed Signature and depicted it in the painting, but it took longer to get an approval on exactly where the names would go on the hood. In the meantime, I had to finish "LMS 2000" and get it to the program printer, so out the door it went minus signatures.

In fact, even after the decision was made, Jeff drove the car one week with the signatures and one week without them.

On a different note, I enjoyed drawing the sprint car that appears in the painting to promote the speedway's dirt track events, as it gave me a different type of car to work with. It's always exciting for me to occasionally get to paint other forms of motorsports.

"Bristol 2000"

17" x 19", Bristol, 2000

Working in the static realm of paintings has some strong limitations when compared to other media. For example, when a film editor wants to show the progression of time, he splices together a series of images that run from somewhere in the past to present day.

Unfortunately, I don't have that luxury. My images are frozen in time, with no rewind or fast-forward buttons. For me to depict a temporal movement requires tremendous planning and execution of elements like composition, foreground/background interaction, sharpness of focus, and subtleties of shading. In short, I'm using a flat, finite space—the canvas or program cover—to portray progress through the dimension of time.

Working on a project that covers decades has gotten easier because I've been asked to do quite a few of them in my career. One of my favorites is the painting that appeared on the cover of the 2000 Bristol spring race program.

The track's request was that I move the viewer from the late '60s through to present day, highlighting various Bristol winners. After considering a few different approaches, I decided to span the years through the use of some astronomy.

The driving force of the image is a comet flying through the night sky and passing the planets of our solar system. Dale Earnhardt Jr., who was certainly the forerunner of a new wave of drivers in his rookie year of 2000, is leading the comet. A galaxy of Bristol luminaries follows—David Pearson, Darrell Waltrip, Cale Yarborough, and Dale Earnhardt represent a rapid progression through the decades. Along with Dale Jr., Tony Stewart, who had won three races during his 1999 rookie season and captured the summer Bristol pole, represented the aggressive young drivers.

This group of drivers had been specifically requested, but when the painting was finished, someone realized that the inclusion of Tony's Home Depot sponsorship had become a contractual conflict given the the Speedway Motorsports Inc. deal with Lowe's Home Improvement Warehouse. There was no time to physically alter the painting itself, so I quickly created a separate illustration of Bobby Labonte's car and had it scanned and inserted by computer to the image. Everything was shipped to the printer digitally.

Total turnaround time on deadline: about 14 hours!

It's not uncommon for a sponsor obligation to require a last-minute change in something I've painted, and I'm sure this won't be the last time I'll have to work a driver, car, or logo into or out of an image.

Since my commission from the Bristol track did not include purchase of the original painting, I have never modified it to reflect the program cover changes. It continues to hang in my gallery with Tony Stewart in place.

Above: The altered cover shows Bobby Labonte's Interstate Batteries-sponsored car substituted for the Home Depot car of Tony Stewart.

"Family Drive-In"

23" x 20", Charlotte, 2002

In 2002 Lowe's Motor Speedway asked me to create two different covers for its spring races, one for The Winston and one for the Coca-Cola Racing Family 600. Although it meant a lot more work for me at an already busy time of year, I thought it was a great idea because it stressed to fans that the two races were really stand-alone events. In fact, years earlier I had encouraged the track to do two covers. Be careful what you wish for!

Coinciding with this decision was a new format for The Winston. Now, the folks at RJ Reynolds have done a great job building the maximum amount of excitement into their all-star, invitation-only race over the years—tweaks and rule changes here and there ensuring it's never the same event twice—but I was especially inspired artistically by the 2002 scheme.

The popular three-segment format was retained, but with a new twist: The field of 27 or so drivers would be narrowed to the top 20 finishers for the second leg, with only 10 cars moving on to the final no-holds-barred shootout. On reading the new rules, I immediately saw a similarity to the hit reality television show "Survivor," in which a group of participants go through torturous contests and ordeals, while gradually voting everyone off of the island until one person—the winner—is left.

In place of Charlotte's state-of-the-art Musco lighting system, I suggested Tiki torches would illuminate the night race. In silhouette you see the event's sole survivor standing on his car with the distinctive crystal Winston trophy held high in triumph. Behind and above the symbolic victory lane scene is a cavalcade of roaring Winston Cup cars with Hendrick teammates Jeff Gordon and Jimmie Johnson leading a tightly packed train to the finish line.

For the Coca-Cola Racing Family 600, I chose to launch a new idea I had that blends the screaming excitement of stock car racing with the laid-back nostalgic mood of a 1950s drive-in restaurant. "Family Drive-In" depicts the Coca-Cola Racing Family of drivers slowing down after 600 hard miles behind the wheel to enjoy a burger and Coke in LMS' infield. The drive-in in my painting is a '50s-style-yet-futuristic neon-wrapped dream firing twin spotlight beams into space through lamps shaped like giant Coca-Cola bottles. The parking lot is packed with NASCAR's most recognizable rides, including the cars of Bobby Labonte, Kevin Harvick, Dale Jarrett, Michael Waltrip, and Bill Elliott.

"Family Drive-In" turned out awesome, and Humpy Wheeler even joked that the painting looked so realistic he might have to ultimately build such a place in the infield. That motif of the family drive-in and the nostalgic feel is something I plan to carry through to a number of paintings in the future for both the Coca-Cola race and other events.

"Family Drive-In" had a small conflict to work around. One of the key drivers in that painting is Tony Stewart, who would win the championship that year. Coca-Cola, the sponsor of the race, wanted a strong display of all the cars that represent their "family," but Lowe's Home Improvement Warehouse—the title sponsor of the track—of course did not want Stewart's Home Depot car shown. I arrived at a way to crop the illustration strategically so all you saw of Tony's car was a side view from the nose to just behind the number 20.

By showing the car from the side—and there were all angles and views of cars in this illustration—it wasn't obvious what I was trying to accomplish. It just looked like his car was pulling into the frame, as you would expect in any painting or photo of a busy diner. I was quite proud to be able to get his car on the cover in such a way that was acceptable to everyone involved.

Looking back on these two paintings, I'm amazed at how much work I managed to get done in just two weeks. The Winston painting required a large number of cars be displayed; otherwise, the "whittling down" theme of the race would not be suggested. I illustrated 11 in all.

Coincidentally, the drive-in scene I created for the Coca-Cola Racing Family 600 also required 11 cars, because that's how many the sponsor had signed on for its promotion. In all, I painted 22 cars in two weeks. I felt like the Earl Scheib of racing!

"Draw!"

22" x 19", Charlotte, 2002

By October 2002 the intensity of the championship points race had reached a new high. Perhaps generating the most excitement was the fact that three of the top five drivers were relative newcomers who managed to pull ahead of their more established teammates.

The battle between the young guns and seasoned veterans—the overriding, unofficial theme of the 2002 season to that point—was my inspiration for the fall Charlotte race program cover. It also gave me an excuse to use one of my favorite settings for a painting—the Wild West.

Two gunslingers face off in an Old West desert location backed up by their automotive gangs. Representing the hungry young drivers are the cars of Matt Kenseth, Jimmie Johnson, Dale Earnhardt Jr., Ryan Newman, and Kevin Harvick. The mature, experienced bunch includes Jeff Gordon, Bill Elliott, Dale Jarrett, Rusty Wallace, and Sterling Marlin.

One of the veteran drivers inclusion in this painting makes it something of a historical bookmark. Sterling Marlin, for whom 2002 was shaping up to be a championship season, was sidelined due to injury just as "Draw!" went to the program printer. His replacement, Jamie McMurray, won that Charlotte race in only his second Winston Cup career race! In doing so, he broke the previous record set by Kevin Harvick, who had won his third Cup race just a year before in Atlanta.

"Most Wanted!"

17" x 22", Texas, 2003

For the 2003 Texas Motor Speedway race program cover, I combined several of my favorite themes and compositional styles.

I enjoy working with a Wild West theme, a given considering TMS's location, and I like for my paintings to tell a story whenever possible, so the viewer can spend more time with one of my illustrations than they could if they were simply looking at a photograph. With portraits of all six previous race winners, done in a sepia pen and ink on a "Wanted" poster format, the painting is a celebration of the short but colorful history of the Texas track.

The portraits make up the centerpiece of the illustration, with the background being a blue sky with hints of the flags of the United States and Texas. Given the impending war in Iraq, I knew the patriotic feelings of those attending the race would be very high.

I positioned the current cars of the six former race champions so they appeared to be driving onto the cover, which gives the image a real three-dimensional quality that tricks the eye just a bit.

After putting 140 hours into "Most Wanted!" I can honestly say I would put it on my list of favorite paintings. Of course, I always enjoy working for the Texas track because I get to portray a range of cars—not only Winston Cup and Busch, but Indy cars and trucks as well over their season's events.

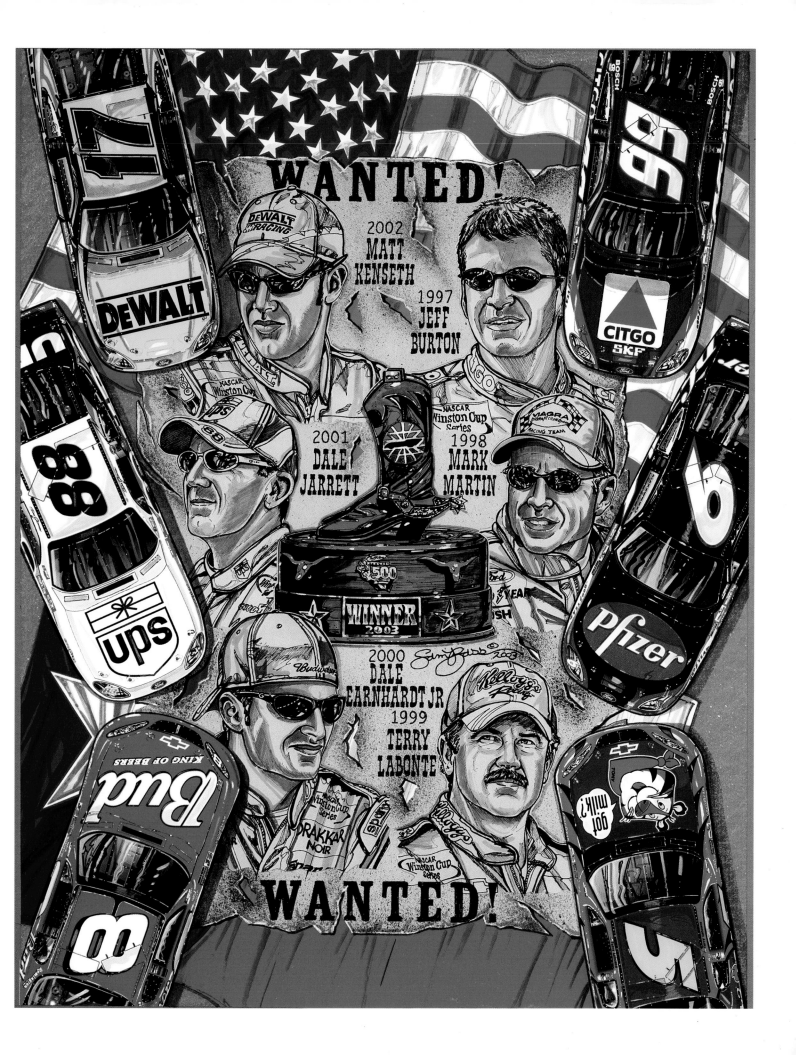

EPILOGUE

There's no doubt I've put together a dream job for myself, but most of the time it's far from anyone's definition of glamorous. I have to laugh when people comment that they would give anything to have my job. I'm pretty sure, having stood many times on the other side of the garage fence myself in the early days, that many race fans must think my days consist of lunches with NASCAR champions and cocktails with team owners.

The average painting takes a minimum of 80 hours to complete, but some represent 300 to 400 hours. Every piece of artwork and design that leaves my studio is a personal production, and I wouldn't have it any other way. For me, 16- and 18-hour days are common. Like any motivated business owner, my lunches often consist of drive-through food, or a salad that I eat at my desk or drawing table. If I'm lucky to have dinner at a reasonable hour, I'm happiest when it's with my family. Weekends…well, weekends when I'm not at a racetrack —usually find me in the studio with the phone turned off, deep in thought over a project.

Despite the long hours and the hard work, it's a great job. I'm doing what I love, and I am fortunate to work with the most exciting people in racing and the most passionate fans in all of motorsports. From the very beginning, my objective has always been to paint something special for the fan in me, and to share it with other fans. That's what drives me and excites me about the projects I do.

One of the biggest compliments I get is when fans look at my paintings and say to me, "I can really tell in your art that you love what you're doing." I don't know exactly how that emotional quality comes through in my painting, but I hear those comments constantly, and they make me very proud. And when drivers tell me that they really appreciate what I do, that's the greatest thing in the world, because they are my heroes.